The Lectionary
2022

First published in Great Britain in 2021

Society for Promoting Christian Knowledge
36 Causton Street
London SW1P 4ST
www.spck.org.uk

British Library Cataloguing-in-Publication Data
A catalogue record for this book is available from the British Library

ISBN 978-0-281-08537-8
ISBN 978-0-281-08538-5 (spiral-bound)

1 3 5 7 9 10 8 6 4 2

Designed by Colin Hall, Refined Practice
Typeset by Fakenham Prepress Solutions, Fakenham, Norfolk NR21 8NL
Printed in Great Britain by Ashford Colour Press

Produced on paper from sustainable forests

CONTENTS

UNDERSTANDING THE LECTIONARY

Common Worship on left-hand page

		Sunday Principal Service / Weekday Eucharist	Third Service / Morning Prayer	Second Service / Evening Prayer
6 Saturday	**THE TRANSFIGURATION OF OUR LORD**			
w		Dan. 7. 9–10, 13–14 Ps. 97 2 Pet. 1. 16–19 Luke 9. 28–36	*MP*: Ps. 27; 150 Ecclus. 48. 1–10 or 1 Kings 19. 1–16 1 John 3. 1–3	*EP*: Ps. 72 Exod. 34. 29–end 2 Cor. ch. 3
7 Sunday	**THE EIGHTH SUNDAY AFTER TRINITY (Proper 14)**			
G		*Track 1* Isa. 1. 1, 10–20 Ps. 50. 1–8, 23–end (*or* 50. 1–7) Heb. 11. 1–3, 8–16 Luke 12. 32–40	*Track 2* Gen. 15. 1–6 Ps. 33. 12–end (*or* 33. 12–21) Heb. 11. 1–3, 8–16 Luke 12. 32–40	Ps. 115 Song of Sol. 8. 5–7 or 1 Macc. 14. 4–15 2 Pet. 3. 8–13
				Ps. 108; [116] Isa. 11.10 – 12.end 2 Cor. 1. 1–22 *Gospel*: Mark 7. 24–30
8 Monday	**Dominic, Priest, Founder of the Order of Preachers, 1221**			
Gw **DEL 19**		Com. Religious or *also* Ecclus. 39. 1–10	Ezek. 1. 2–5, 24–end Ps. 148. 1–4, 12–13 Matt. 17. 22–end	Ps. 27; **30** 1 Sam. 14. 24–46 Luke 23. 13–25
				Ps. 26; **28**; 29 Jer. 31. 23–25, 27–37 Jas. 2. 1–13

Column 1

- Date
- **Colour:** An upper-case letter indicates the liturgical colour of the day. A lower-case second colour indicates the colour for a Lesser Festival while the upper-case letter indicates the continuing seasonal colour.
- **DEL:** Week number of Daily Eucharistic Lectionary.

Column 2

- Name of the Principal Holy Day, Sunday, Festival or Lesser Festival;
- a note of other Commemorations for mention in prayers;
- any general note that applies to the whole *Common Worship* provision for the day;
- one of the options where there are two options for readings at the Eucharist or Principal Service.

Readings: Readings occur in this column only in two circumstances.

1. **On Sundays after Trinity** where there are two 'tracks' for the Principal Service readings (where there is a choice of first reading and psalm, but the second reading and Gospel are the same in both tracks), Track I appears in this column.

2. **On Lesser Festivals throughout the year** where there are readings for that festival that are alternative to the semi-continuous Daily Eucharistic Lectionary, these also appear in this column.

Column 3

On Principal Feasts, Principal Holy Days, Sundays and Festivals this gives the Principal Service Lectionary, intended for use at the main service of the day (in most churches the mid-morning service), whether or not it is a Eucharist.

On other weekdays this gives the Daily Eucharistic Lectionary for those wanting a semi-continuous pattern of readings and a psalm for Holy Communion. It is most useful in a church where there is a daily celebration and a core community that worships together day by day, though its use is not restricted to that.

Column 4

On Principal Feasts, Principal Holy Days, Sundays and Festivals this gives the Third Service Lectionary. Many churches will have no need of it, for it comes into use only if the Principal and Second Service Lectionaries have been used. Its most likely use is at Morning Prayer (when this is not the Principal Service). Where psalms are recommended for use in the morning, these also appear in this column.

On other weekdays this provides the psalmody and readings for Morning Prayer. Where two or more psalms are appointed, the psalm in bold italic may be used as the only psalm. Psalms printed in round brackets ( ) may be omitted if they are used as an opening canticle at Morning Prayer. Where † is printed after the psalm number, the psalm may be shortened if desired. For those wishing to follow the Ordinary Time psalm cycle throughout the year (except for the period between 19 December and the Epiphany and from the Monday of Holy Week to the Saturday of Easter Week), this is printed as an alternative to the seasonal provision.

Column 5

On Principal Feasts, Principal Holy Days, Sundays and Festivals this gives the Second Service Lectionary, intended for use when a second set of readings is required. Its most likely use is in the evening, when the Principal Service Lectionary has been used in the morning. Sometimes it might be used at an evening Eucharist. Where the second reading is not a Gospel reading, an alternative to meet this need is provided. Where psalms are recommended for use in the evening, these also appear in this column.

On other weekdays this provides the psalmody and readings for Evening Prayer. Where two or more psalms are provided, the psalm in bold italic may be used as the only psalm. Psalms printed in round brackets ( ) may be omitted if they are used as an opening canticle at Evening Prayer. Where † is printed after the psalm number, the psalm may be shortened if desired. For those wishing to follow the Ordinary Time psalm cycle throughout the year (except for the period between 19 December and the Epiphany and from the Monday of Holy Week to the Saturday of Easter Week), this is printed as an alternative to the seasonal provision.

Book of Common Prayer

August 2022

	Calendar and Holy Communion	Morning Prayer	Evening Prayer	NOTES
	THE TRANSFIGURATION OF OUR LORD			
𝖜	Exod. 24. 12–end Ps. 84. 1–7 1 John 3. 1–3 Mark 9. 2–7	(Ps. 27; 150) Ecclus. 48. 1–10 *or* 1 Kings 19. 1–16 2 Pet. 1. 16–19	(Ps. 72) Exod. 34. 29–end 2 Cor. ch. 3	
	THE EIGHTH SUNDAY AFTER TRINITY			
G	Jer. 23. 16–24 Ps. 31. 1–6 Rom. 8. 12–17 Matt. 7. 15–21	Ps. 115 Song of Sol. 8. 5–7 *or* 1 Macc. 14. 4–15 2 Pet. 3. 8–13	Ps. 108; [116] Isa. 11.10 – 12.end 2 Cor. 1. 1–22	
G		1 Sam. 14. 24–46 Luke 23. 13–25	Jer. 31. 23–25, 27–37 Jas. 2. 1–13	

Column 6

- Liturgical colour (**see** *column 1*).

Column 7

- The name of the Principal Holy Day, Sunday, Festival or Lesser Festival;
- any general note that applies to the whole Prayer Book provision for the day and an indication of points at which users may wish to draw on *Common Worship* material on the opposite page where the BCP has no provision;
- the Lectionary for the Eucharist on any day for which provision is made.

Column 8

This provides the readings for Morning Prayer, together with psalm provision where it varies from the BCP monthly cycle.

Column 9

This provides the readings for Evening Prayer, together with psalm provision where it varies from the BCP monthly cycle.

A letter to indicate liturgical colour in this column indicates a change of colour for Evening Prayer. The symbol in bold lower case, **ct**, indicates that the Collect at Evening Prayer should be that of the following day. This also applies to Column 5.

Column 10

Space for notes.

ABBREVIATIONS OF BOOKS OF THE BIBLE

Old Testament

Gen. (Genesis)	Kings	Song of Sol. (Song of Solomon)	Obad. (Obadiah)
Exod. (Exodus)	Chron. (Chronicles)	Isa. (Isaiah)	Jonah
Lev. (Leviticus)	Ezra	Jer. (Jeremiah)	Mic. (Micah)
Num. (Numbers)	Neh. (Nehemiah)	Lam. (Lamentations)	Nahum
Deut. (Deuteronomy)	Esth. (Esther)	Ezek. (Ezekiel)	Hab. (Habakkuk)
Josh. (Joshua)	Job	Dan. (Daniel)	Zeph. (Zephaniah)
Judg. (Judges)	Ps. (Psalms)	Hos. (Hosea)	Hag. (Haggai)
Ruth	Prov. (Proverbs)	Joel	Zech. (Zechariah)
Sam. (Samuel)	Eccles. (Ecclesiastes)	Amos	Mal. (Malachi)

Apocrypha

Esd. (Esdras)	Wisd. (Wisdom of Solomon)	Song of the Three (Song of the	Prayer of Manasseh
Tobit	Ecclus. (Ecclesiasticus)	Three Children)	Macc. (Maccabees)
Judith	Baruch	Susanna (The History of Susanna)	

New Testament

Matt. (Matthew)	Cor. (Corinthians)	Tim. (Timothy)	John (letters of John)
Mark	Gal. (Galatians)	Titus	Jude
Luke	Eph. (Ephesians)	Philem. (Philemon)	Rev. (Revelation)
John	Phil. (Philippians)	Heb. (Hebrews)	
Acts (Acts of the Apostles)	Col. (Colossians)	Jas. (James)	
Rom. (Romans)	Thess. (Thessalonians)	Pet. (Peter)	

MAKING CHOICES IN *COMMON WORSHIP*

Common Worship makes provision for a variety of pastoral and liturgical circumstances. It needs to, for it has to serve some church communities where Morning Prayer, Holy Communion and Evening Prayer are all celebrated every day, and yet be useful also in a church with only one service a week, and that service varying in form and time from week to week.

At the beginning of the year, some decisions in principle need to be taken.

In relation to the Calendar, whether to keep The Epiphany on Thursday 6 January or on Sunday 2 January, whether to keep The Presentation of Christ (Candlemas) on Wednesday 2 February or on Sunday 30 January, and whether to keep the Feast of All Saints on Tuesday 1 November or on Sunday 30 October.

In relation to the Lectionary, the initial choices every year to decide in relation to Sundays are:

- which of the services on a Principal Feast, Principal Holy Day, Sunday or Festival constitutes the 'Principal Service'; then use the Principal Service Lectionary (column 3) consistently for that service through the year;

- during the Sundays after Trinity, whether to use Track I of the Principal Service Lectionary (column 2), where the first reading stays over several weeks with one Old Testament book read semi-continuously, or Track 2 (column 3), where the first reading is chosen for its relationship to the Gospel reading of the day;

- which, if any, service on a Principal Feast, Principal Holy Day, Sunday or Festival constitutes the 'Second Service'; then use the Second Service Lectionary (column 5) consistently for that service through the year;

- which, if any, service on a Principal Feast, Principal Holy Day, Sunday or Festival constitutes the 'Third Service'; then use the Third Service Lectionary (column 4) consistently for that service through the year.

And in relation to weekdays:

- whether to use the Daily Eucharistic Lectionary (column 3) consistently for weekday celebrations of Holy Communion (with the exception of Principal Feasts, Principal Holy Days and Festivals) or to make some use of the Lesser Festival provision;

- whether to follow the first psalm provision in column 4 (morning) and column 5 (evening), where psalms during the seasons have a seasonal flavour but in ordinary time follow a sequential pattern; or to follow the alternative provision in the same columns, where psalms follow the sequential pattern throughout the year, except for the period between 19 December and The Epiphany and from the Monday of Holy Week to the Saturday of Easter Week; or to follow the psalm cycle in the Book of Common Prayer, where they are nearly always used 'in course';

- whether to use the Additional Weekday Lectionary (which begins on page 116) for weekday services (other than Holy Communion). It provides a one-year cycle of two readings for each day (except for Sundays, Principal Feasts, Principal Holy Days, Festivals and during Holy Week). Since each of the readings is designed to 'stand alone' (that is, it is complete in itself and will make sense to the worshipper who has not attended on the previous day and who will not be present on the next day), it is intended particularly for use in those churches and cathedrals that attract occasional rather than regular congregations.

The flexibility of *Common Worship* is intended to enable the church and the minister to find the most helpful provision for them. But once a decision is made, it is advisable to stay with that decision through the year or at the very least through a complete season.

All Bible references (except to the psalms) are to the New Revised Standard Version, Anglicized edition (1995). Those who use other Bible translations should check the verse numbers against the NRSV. References to the psalms are to the *Common Worship* Psalter.

BOOK OF COMMON PRAYER

A separate Lectionary for the Book of Common Prayer is no longer issued. Provision is made on the right-hand pages of this Lectionary for BCP worship on all Sundays in the year, for the major festivals and for Morning and Evening Prayer. The Epistles and Gospels for Holy Communion are those of 1662, with the additions and variations of 1928, now authorized under the *Common Worship* overall provision. The Old Testament readings and psalms for these services, formerly appended to the Series One Holy Communion service, may be used but are not mandatory with the 1662 order.

Readings for Morning and Evening Prayer, which are the same as those for *Common Worship*, are set out in the BCP section for Sundays and weekdays. The special psalm provision of the BCP is given; however, where the *Common Worship* psalm provision is used, verse numbering may occasionally differ slightly from that in the BCP Psalter, and appropriate adjustment will have to be made (a table of variations in verse numbering can be found at www.churchofengland.org/prayer-and-worship/worship-texts-and-resources/common-worship/daily-prayer/psalter/psalter-verse). Otherwise the Psalter is read in course daily through each month.

The Calendar observes BCP dates when these differ from those of *Common Worship*; for example, St Thomas on 21 December. Additional commemorations in the *Common Worship* Calendar are not included, but those who wish to observe them may use the *Collects and Post Communions in Traditional Language: Lesser Festivals, Common of the Saints, Special Occasions* (Church House Publishing).

The Lectionaries of 1871 and 1922, to be found in many copies of the BCP, are still authorized and may be used, but – with the exception of the psalms and readings for Holy Communion mentioned above – the Additional Alternative Lectionary (1961) is no longer authorized for public worship.

Although those who use the BCP, for private or public worship or both, are free to follow any of the authorized lectionaries, there is much to be said for common usage across the Church of England, so that the same passages are being read by all. It is of course appropriate that BCP readings should be taken from the Authorized or King James Version for harmony of style, with the daily recitation of the BCP Psalter.

The integrity of the BCP as the traditional source of worship in the Church of England is not in any way affected by the use of a common lectionary for the daily offices.

CERTAIN DAYS AND OCCASIONS COMMONLY OBSERVED

Plough Sunday may be observed on 9 January 2022.

The Week of Prayer for Christian Unity may be observed from 18 to 25 January 2022.

Education Sunday may be observed on 11 September 2022.

Rogation Sunday may be observed on 22 May 2022.

The Feast of Dedication is observed on the anniversary of the dedication or consecration of a church, or, when the actual date is unknown, on 2 October 2022. In *Common Worship*, 23 October 2022 is an alternative date.

Ember Days. *Common Worship* encourages the bishop to set the Ember Days in each diocese in the week before the ordinations, whereas in BCP the dates are fixed.

Days of Discipline and Self-Denial in *Common Worship* are the weekdays of Lent and all Fridays in the year, except all Principal Feasts and festivals outside Lent and Fridays between Easter Day and Pentecost. The eves of Principal Feasts are also appropriately kept as days of discipline and self-denial in preparation for the feast.

Days of Fasting and Abstinence according to the BCP are the forty days of Lent, the Ember Days at the four seasons, the three Rogation Days, and all Fridays in the year except Christmas Day. The BCP also orders the observance of the Evens or Vigils before The Nativity of our Lord, The Purification of the Blessed Virgin Mary, The Annunciation of the Blessed Virgin Mary, Easter Day, Ascension Day, Pentecost, and before the following saints' days: Matthias, John the Baptist, Peter, James, Bartholomew, Matthew, Simon and Jude, Andrew, Thomas, and All Saints. (If any of these days falls on Monday, the Vigil is to be kept on the previous Saturday.)

KEY TO LITURGICAL COLOURS

Common Worship suggests appropriate liturgical colours. They are not mandatory, and traditional or local use may be followed.

For a detailed discussion of when colours may be used, see *Common Worship: Services and Prayers for the Church of England* (Church House Publishing), *New Handbook of Pastoral Liturgy* (SPCK) or *A Companion to Common Worship: Volume I* (SPCK).

When a lower-case letter accompanies an upper-case letter, the lower-case letter indicates the liturgical colour appropriate to the Lesser Festival of that day, while the upper-case letter indicates the continuing seasonal colour.

W White
w Gold or white
R Red
P Purple (may vary from 'Roman purple' to violet, with blue as an alternative; a Lent array of sackcloth may be used in Lent, and rose pink on The Third Sunday of Advent and Fourth Sunday of Lent)
G Green

PRINCIPAL FEASTS, HOLY DAYS AND FESTIVALS

Principal Feasts and other Principal Holy Days (Ash Wednesday, Maundy Thursday, Good Friday) are printed in **LARGE BOLD CAPITALS** in the Lectionary.

There are no longer proper readings relating to the Holy Spirit on the six days after Pentecost. Instead they have been located on the nine days before Pentecost.

When Patronal and Dedication Festivals are kept as Principal Feasts, they may be transferred to the nearest Sunday, unless that day is already either a Principal Feast or The First Sunday of Advent, The Baptism of Christ, The First Sunday of Lent or Palm Sunday.

Festivals are printed in the Lectionary in **SMALL BOLD CAPITALS**.

For each day there is a full liturgical provision for the Holy Communion and for Morning and Evening Prayer. Most holy days that are in the category 'Festival' are provided with an optional First Evening Prayer. Its use is entirely at the discretion of the minister. Where it is used, the liturgical colour for the next day should be used at that First Evening Prayer, and this has been indicated in the provision on the following pages.

LESSER FESTIVALS AND COMMEMORATIONS

Lesser Festivals (printed in **medium-bold roman** typeface) are observed at the level appropriate to a particular church. The readings and psalms for The Common of the Saints are listed on page 10. In addition, there are special readings appropriate to the Festival listed in the first column. The daily psalms and readings at Morning and Evening Prayer are not usually superseded by those for Lesser Festivals, but the readings and psalms for Holy Communion may on occasion be used at Morning or Evening Prayer.

Commemorations are printed in the Lectionary in *italic* typeface. They do not have collect, psalm or readings, but may be observed by mention in prayers of intercession and thanksgiving. For local reasons,

or where there is an established tradition in the wider Church, they may be kept as Lesser Festivals using the appropriate material from The Common of the Saints. Equally, it may be desirable to observe some Lesser Festivals as Commemorations.

If a Lesser Festival or a Commemoration falls on a Principal Feast, Principal Holy Day, Sunday or Festival, it is not normally observed that year, although it may be celebrated, where there is sufficient reason, on the nearest available day. Lesser Festivals and Commemorations which, for this reason, would not be celebrated in 2021–22 are listed on pages 9–10, so that, if desired, they may be mentioned in prayers of intercession and thanksgiving.

LESSER FESTIVALS AND COMMEMORATIONS NOT OBSERVED IN 2021–22

The Lesser Festivals and Commemorations (shown in italics) listed below fall on a Sunday or during Holy Week or Easter Week this year, and are thus not observed in this Lectionary.

COMMON WORSHIP

2022

January

2 Basil the Great and Gregory of Nazianzus, Bishops, Teachers, 379 and 389
  Seraphim, Monk of Sarov, Spiritual Guide, 1833
  Vedanayagam Samuel Azariah, Bishop in South India, Evangelist, 1945
30 Charles, King and Martyr, 1649

February

6 *The Martyrs of Japan, 1597*
27 George Herbert, Priest, Poet, 1633

March

2 Chad, Bishop of Lichfield, Missionary, 672

April

10 William Law, Priest, Spiritual Writer, 1761
  William of Ockham, Friar, Philosopher, Teacher, 1347
11 *George Augustus Selwyn, first Bishop of New Zealand, 1878*
16 *Isabella Gilmore, Deaconess, 1923*
19 Alphege, Archbishop of Canterbury, Martyr, 1012
21 Anselm, Abbot of Le Bec, Archbishop of Canterbury, Teacher, 1109
24 *Mellitus, Bishop of London, first Bishop of St Paul's, 624*
  The Seven Martyrs of the Melanesian Brotherhood, Solomon Islands, 2003

May

2 Athanasius, Bishop of Alexandria, Teacher, 373
8 Julian of Norwich, Spiritual Writer, c. 1417
26 Augustine, first Archbishop of Canterbury, 605

June

5 Boniface (Wynfrith) of Crediton, Bishop, Apostle of Germany, Martyr, 754
19 *Sundar Singh of India, Sadhu (holy man), Evangelist, Teacher, 1929*

July

31 *Ignatius of Loyola, Founder of the Society of Jesus, 1556*

August

7 *John Mason Neale, Priest, Hymn Writer, 1866*
14 *Maximilian Kolbe, Friar, Martyr, 1941*
28 Augustine, Bishop of Hippo, Teacher, 430

September

4 *Birinus, Bishop of Dorchester (Oxon), Apostle of Wessex, 650*
25 Lancelot Andrewes, Bishop of Winchester, Spiritual Writer, 1626
  Sergei of Radonezh, Russian Monastic Reformer, Teacher, 1392

October

9 *Denys, Bishop of Paris, and his Companions, Martyrs, c. 250*
  Robert Grosseteste, Bishop of Lincoln, Philosopher, Scientist, 1253

November

6 *Leonard, Hermit, 6th century*
  William Temple, Archbishop of Canterbury, Teacher, 1944
13 Charles Simeon, Priest, Evangelical Divine, 1836
20 Edmund, King of the East Angles, Martyr, 870
  Priscilla Lydia Sellon, a Restorer of the Religious Life in the Church of England, 1876

December

4 *John of Damascus, Monk, Teacher, c. 749*
  Nicholas Ferrar, Deacon, Founder of the Little Gidding Community, 1637

BOOK OF COMMON PRAYER

2022

January
30 Charles, King and Martyr, 1649

March
2 Chad, Bishop of Lichfield, Missionary, 672

April
3 Richard, Bishop of Chichester, 1253
19 Alphege, Archbishop of Canterbury, Martyr, 1012

May
26 Augustine, first Archbishop of Canterbury, 605

June
5 Boniface (Wynfrith) of Crediton, Bishop, Apostle of Germany, Martyr, 754

August
7 The Name of Jesus
28 Augustine, Bishop of Hippo, Teacher, 430

October
9 Denys, Bishop of Paris, and his Companions, Martyrs, c. 250

November
6 Leonard, Hermit, 6th century
13 Britius, Bishop of Tours, 444
20 Edmund, King of the East Angles, Martyr, 870

THE COMMON OF THE SAINTS

The Blessed Virgin Mary
Genesis 3. 8–15, 20; Isaiah 7. 10–14; Micah 5. 1–4
Psalms 45. 10–17; 113; 131
Acts 1. 12–14; Romans 8. 18–30; Galatians 4. 4–7
Luke 1. 26–38; I. 39–47; John 19. 25–27

Martyrs
2 Chronicles 24. 17–21; Isaiah 43. 1–7;
    Jeremiah 11. 18–20; Wisdom 4. 10–15
Psalms 3; 11; 31. 1–5; 44. 18–24; 126
Romans 8. 35–end; 2 Corinthians 4. 7–15;
    2 Timothy 2. 3–7 [8–13]; Hebrews 11. 32–end;
    1 Peter 4. 12–end; Revelation 12. 10–12a
Matthew 10. 16–22; 10. 28–39; 16. 24–26;
    John 12. 24–26; 15. 18–21

Teachers of the Faith and Spiritual Writers
I Kings 3. [6–10] 11–14; Proverbs 4. 1–9;
    Wisdom 7. 7–10, 15–16; Ecclesiasticus 39. 1–10
Psalms 19. 7–10; 34. 11–17; 37. 31–35; 119. 89–96;
    119. 97–104
I Corinthians 1. 18–25; 2. 1–10; 2. 9–end;
    Ephesians 3. 8–12; 2 Timothy 4. 1–8; Titus 2. 1–8
Matthew 5. 13–19; 13. 52–end; 23. 8–12; Mark 4. 1–9;
    John 16. 12–15

Bishops and Other Pastors
I Samuel 16. I, 6–13; Isaiah 6. 1–8; Jeremiah 1. 4–10;
    Ezekiel 3. 16–21; Malachi 2. 5–7
Psalms 1; 15; 16. 5–end; 96; 110
Acts 20. 28–35; I Corinthians 4. 1–5;
    2 Corinthians 4. 1–10 (or 1–2, 5–7);
    5. 14–20; 1 Peter 5. 1–4

Matthew 11. 25–end; 24. 42–46; John 10. 11–16;
    15. 9–17; 21. 15–17

Members of Religious Communities
I Kings 19. 9–18; Proverbs 10. 27–end;
    Song of Solomon 8. 6–7; Isaiah 61.10 – 62.5;
    Hosea 2. 14–15, 19–20
Psalms 34. 1–8; 112. 1–9; 119. 57–64; 123; 131
Acts 4. 32–35; 2 Corinthians 10.17 – 11.2;
    Philippians 3. 7–14; 1 John 2. 15–17;
    Revelation 19. 1, 5–9
Matthew 11. 25–end; 19. 3–12; 19. 23–end;
    Luke 9. 57–end; 12. 32–37

Missionaries
Isaiah 52. 7–10; 61. 1–3a; Ezekiel 34. 11–16; Jonah 3. 1–5
Psalms 67; 87; 97; 100; 117
Acts 2. 14, 22–36; 13. 46–49; 16. 6–10; 26. 19–23;
    Romans 15. 17–21; 2 Corinthians 5.11 – 6.2
Matthew 9. 35–end; 28. 16–end; Mark 16. 15–20;
    Luke 5. 1–11; 10. 1–9

Any Saint
Genesis 12. 1–4; Proverbs 8. 1–11; Micah 6. 6–8;
    Ecclesiasticus 2. 7–13 [14–end]
Psalms 32; 33. 1–5; 119. 1–8; 139. 1–4 [5–12]; 145. 8–14
Ephesians 3. 14–19; 6. 11–18; Hebrews 13. 7–8, 15–16;
    James 2. 14–17; 1 John 4. 7–16; Revelation 21. [1–4]
    5–7
Matthew 19. 16–21; 25. 1–13; 25. 14–30; John 15. 1–8;
    17. 20–end

SPECIAL OCCASIONS

The Guidance of the Holy Spirit
Proverbs 24. 3–7; Isaiah 30. 15–21; Wisdom 9. 13–17
Psalms 25. 1–9; 104. 26–33; 143. 8–10
Acts 15. 23–29; Romans 8. 22–27;
   1 Corinthians 12. 4–13
Luke 14. 27–33; John 14. 23–26; 16. 13–15

The Commemoration of the Faithful Departed
Lamentations 3. 17–26, 31–33 or Wisdom 3. 1–9
Psalm 23 or 27. 1–6, 16–end
Romans 5. 5–11 or I Peter 1. 3–9
John 5. 19–25 or 6. 37–40

Rogation Days
Deuteronomy 8. 1–10; 1 Kings 8. 35–40; Job 28. 1–11
Psalms 104. 21–30; 107. 1–9; 121
Philippians 4. 4–7; 2 Thessalonians 3. 6–13;
   1 John 5. 12–15
Matthew 6. 1–15; Mark 11. 22–24; Luke 11. 5–13

Harvest Thanksgiving

Year A
Deuteronomy 8. 7–18 or 28. 1–14
Psalm 65
2 Corinthians 9. 6–end
Luke 12. 16–30 or 17. 11–19

Year B
Joel 2. 21–27
Psalm 126
1 Timothy 2. 1–7 or 6. 6–10
Matthew 6. 25–33

Year C
Deuteronomy 26. 1–11
Psalm 100
Philippians 4. 4–9 or Revelation 14. 14–18
John 6. 25–35

Mission and Evangelism
Isaiah 49. 1–6; 52. 7–10; Micah 4. 1–5
Psalms 2; 46; 67
Acts 17. 12–end; 2 Corinthians 5.14 - 6.2;
   Ephesians 2. 13–end
Matthew 5. 13–16; 28. 16–end; John 17. 20–end

The Unity of the Church
Jeremiah 33. 6–9a; Ezekiel 36. 23–28;
   Zephaniah 3. 16–end
Psalms 100; 122; 133
Ephesians 4. 1–6; Colossians 3. 9–17;
   1 John 4. 9–15
Matthew 18. 19–22; John 11. 45–52; 17. 11b–23

The Peace of the World
Isaiah 9. 1–6; 57. 15–19; Micah 4. 1–5
Psalms 40. 14–17; 72. 1–7; 85. 8–13
Philippians 4. 6–9; 1 Timothy 2. 1–6;
   James 3. 13–18
Matthew 5. 43–end; John 14. 23–29; 15. 9–17

Social Justice and Responsibility
Isaiah 32. 15–end; Amos 5. 21–24; 8. 4–7;
   Acts 5. 1–11
Psalms 31. 1–24; 85. 1–7; 146. 5–10
Colossians 3. 12–15; James 2. 1–4
Matthew 5. 1–12; 25. 31–end;
   Luke 16. 19–end

Ministry (including Ember Days)
Numbers 11. 16–17, 24–29; 27. 15–end;
   1 Samuel 16. 1–13a; Isaiah 6. 1–8; 61. 1–3;
   Jeremiah 1. 4–10
Psalms 40. 8–13; 84. 8–12; 89. 19–25;
   101. 1–5, 7; 122
Acts 20. 28–35; 1 Corinthians 3. 3–11;
   Ephesians 4. 4–16; Philippians 3. 7–14
Luke 4. 16–21; 12. 35–43; 22. 24–27;
   John 4. 31–38; 15. 5–17

In Time of Trouble
Genesis 9. 8–17; Job 1. 13–end; Isaiah 38. 6–11
Psalms 86. 1–7; 107. 4–15; 142. 1–7
Romans 3. 21–26; 8. 18–25;
   2 Corinthians 8. 1–5, 9
Mark 4. 35–end; Luke 12. 1–7; John 16. 31–end

For the Sovereign
Joshua 1. 1–9; Proverbs 8. 1–16
Psalms 20; 101; 121
Romans 13. 1–10; Revelation 21.22 - 22.4
Matthew 22. 16–22; Luke 22. 24–30

		Sunday Principal Service Weekday Eucharist	Third Service Morning Prayer	Second Service Evening Prayer
28 Sunday	**THE FIRST SUNDAY OF ADVENT** *Common Worship* Year C begins			
P		Jer. 33. 14–16 Ps. 25. 1–9 1 Thess. 3. 9–end Luke 21. 25–36	Ps. 44 Isa. 51. 4–11 Rom. 13. 11–end	Ps. 9 (*or* 9. 1–8) Joel 3. 9–end Rev. 14.13 – 15.4 *Gospel:* John 3. 1–17
29 Monday	Daily Eucharistic Lectionary Year 2 begins			
P		Isa. 2. 1–5 Ps. 122 Matt. 8. 5–11	Ps. *50*; 54 *alt.* Ps. *1*; 2; 3 Isa. 25. 1–9 Matt. 12. 1–21	Ps. 70; *71* *alt.* Ps. *4*; 7 Isa. 42. 18–end Rev. ch. 19 *or First EP of Andrew* *the Apostle* Ps. 48 Isa. 49. 1–9a 1 Cor. 4. 9–16 **R ct**

Day of Intercession and Thanksgiving for the Missionary Work of the Church

Isa. 49. 1–6; Isa. 52. 7–10; Mic. 4. 1–5
Acts 17. 12–end; 2 Cor. 5.14 – 6.2; Eph. 2. 13–end
Ps. 2; 46; 47
Matt. 5. 13–16; Matt. 28. 16–end; John 17. 20–end

30 Tuesday	**ANDREW THE APOSTLE**			
R		Isa. 52. 7–10 Ps. 19. 1–6 Rom. 10. 12–18 Matt. 4. 18–22	*MP*: Ps. 47; 147. 1–12 Ezek. 47. 1–12 *or* Ecclus. 14. 20–end John 12. 20–32	*EP*: Ps. 87; 96 Zech. 8. 20–end John 1. 35–42

December 2021

1 Wednesday	*Charles de Foucauld, Hermit in the Sahara, 1916*			
P		Isa. 25. 6–10a Ps. 23 Matt. 15. 29–37	Ps. 5; *7* *alt.* Ps. 119. 1–32 Isa. 28. 1–13 Matt. 12. 38–end	Ps. 76; *77* *alt.* Ps. *11*; 12; 13 Isa. 43. 14–end Rev. 21. 1–8
2 Thursday				
P		Isa. 26. 1–6 Ps. 118. 18–27a Matt. 7. 21, 24–27	Ps. *42*; 43 *alt.* Ps. 14; *15*; 16 Isa. 28. 14–end Matt. 13. 1–23	Ps. *40*; 46 *alt.* Ps. 18† Isa. 44. 1–8 Rev. 21. 9–21
3 Friday	*Francis Xavier, Missionary, Apostle of the Indies, 1552*			
P		Isa. 29. 17–end Ps. 27. 1–4, 16–17 Matt. 9. 27–31	Ps. *25*; 26 *alt.* Ps. 17; *19* Isa. 29. 1–14 Matt. 13. 24–43	Ps. 16; *17* *alt.* Ps. 22 Isa. 44. 9–23 Rev. 21.22 – 22.5
4 Saturday	*John of Damascus, Monk, Teacher, c. 749; Nicholas Ferrar, Deacon, Founder of the Little Gidding* *Community, 1637*			
P		Isa. 30. 19–21, 23–26 Ps. 146. 4–9 Matt. 9.35 – 10.1, 6–8	Ps. *9*; (10) *alt.* Ps. 20; 21; *23* Isa. 29. 15–end Matt. 13. 44–end	Ps. *27*; 28 *alt.* Ps. *24*; 25 Isa. 44.24 – 45.13 Rev. 22. 6–end **ct**

	Calendar and Holy Communion	Morning Prayer	Evening Prayer

THE FIRST SUNDAY IN ADVENT
Advent 1 Collect until Christmas Eve

| P | Mic. 4. 1–4, 6–7
Ps. 25. 1–9
Rom. 13. 8–14
Matt. 21. 1–13 | Ps. 44
Isa. 51. 4–11
Rom. 13. 11–end | Ps. 9 (or 9. 1–8)
Joel 3. 9–end
Rev. 14.13 – 15.4 |

| P | | Isa. 25. 1–9
Matt. 12. 1–21 | Isa. 42. 18–end
Rev. ch. 19
or First EP of Andrew
the Apostle
(Ps. 48)
Isa. 49. 1–9a
1 Cor. 4. 9–16 |

R ct

To celebrate the Day of Intercession and Thanksgiving for the Missionary Work of the Church, see *Common Worship* provision.

ANDREW THE APOSTLE

| R | Zech. 8. 20–end
Ps. 92. 1–5
Rom. 10. 9–end
Matt. 4. 18–22 | (Ps. 47; 147. 1–12)
Ezek. 47. 1–12
or Ecclus. 14. 20–end
John 12. 20–32 | (Ps. 87; 96)
Isa. 52. 7–10
John 1. 35–42 |

| P | | Isa. 28. 1–13
Matt. 12. 38–end | Isa. 43. 14–end
Rev. 21. 1–8 |

| P | | Isa. 28. 14–end
Matt. 13. 1–23 | Isa. 44. 1–8
Rev. 21. 9–21 |

| P | | Isa. 29. 1–14
Matt. 13. 24–43 | Isa. 44. 9–23
Rev. 21.22 – 22.5 |

| P | | Isa. 29. 15–end
Matt. 13. 44–end | Isa. 44.24 – 45.13
Rev. 22. 6–end |

ct

		Sunday Principal Service / Weekday Eucharist	Third Service / Morning Prayer	Second Service / Evening Prayer
5 Sunday	THE SECOND SUNDAY OF ADVENT			
P		Baruch ch. 5 / or Mal. 3. 1–4 / Canticle: Benedictus / Phil. 1. 3–11 / Luke 3. 1–6	Ps. 80 / Isa. 64. 1–7 / Matt. 11. 2–11	Ps. 75; [76] / Isa. 40. 1–11 / Luke 1. 1–25
6 Monday	Nicholas, Bishop of Myra, c. 326			
Pw		Com. Bishop or Isa. ch. 35 / also Isa. 61. 1–3 Ps. 85. 7–end / 1 Tim. 6. 6–11 Luke 5. 17–26 / Mark 10. 13–16	Ps. 44 / alt. Ps. 27; **30** / Isa. 30. 1–18 / Matt. 14. 1–12	Ps. **144**; 146 / alt. Ps. 26; **28**; 29 / Isa. 45. 14–end / 1 Thess. ch. 1
7 Tuesday	Ambrose, Bishop of Milan, Teacher, 397			
Pw		Com. Teacher or Isa. 40. 1–11 / also Isa. 41. 9b–13 Ps. 96. 1, 10–end / Luke 22. 24–30 Matt. 18. 12–14	Ps. **56**; 57 / alt. Ps. 32; **36** / Isa. 30. 19–end / Matt. 14. 13–end	Ps. **11**; 12; 13 / alt. Ps. 33 / Isa. ch. 46 / 1 Thess. 2. 1–12
8 Wednesday	The Conception of the Blessed Virgin Mary / Ember Day*			
Pw		Com. BVM or Isa. 40. 25–end / Ps. 103. 8–13 / Matt. 11. 28–end	Ps. **62**; 63 / alt. Ps. 34 / Isa. ch. 31 / Matt. 15. 1–20	Ps. **10**; 14 / alt. Ps. 119. 33–56 / Isa. ch. 47 / 1 Thess. 2. 13–end
9 Thursday				
P		Isa. 41. 13–20 / Ps. 145. 1, 8–13 / Matt. 11. 11–15	Ps. 53; **54**; 60 / alt. Ps. 37† / Isa. ch. 32 / Matt. 15. 21–28	Ps. 73 / alt. Ps. 39; **40** / Isa. 48. 1–11 / 1 Thess. ch. 3
10 Friday	Ember Day*			
P		Isa. 48. 17–19 / Ps. 1 / Matt. 11. 16–19	Ps. 85; **86** / alt. Ps. 31 / Isa. 33. 1–22 / Matt. 15. 29–end	Ps. 82; **90** / alt. Ps. 35 / Isa. 48. 12–end / 1 Thess. 4. 1–12
11 Saturday	Ember Day*			
P		Ecclus. 48. 1–4, 9–11 / or 2 Kings 2. 9–12 / Ps. 80. 1–4, 18–19 / Matt. 17. 10–13	Ps. 145 / alt. Ps. 41; **42**; 43 / Isa. ch. 35 / Matt. 16. 1–12	Ps. 93; **94** / alt. Ps. 45; **46** / Isa. 49. 1–13 / 1 Thess. 4. 13–end / ct
12 Sunday	THE THIRD SUNDAY OF ADVENT			
P		Zeph. 3. 14–end / Canticle: Isa. 12. 2–end / or Ps. 146. 4–end / Phil. 4. 4–7 / Luke 3. 7–18	Ps. 12; 14 / Isa. 25. 1–9 / 1 Cor. 4. 1–5	Ps. 50. 1–6; [62] / Isa. ch. 35 / Luke 1. 57–66 [67–end]
13 Monday	Lucy, Martyr at Syracuse, 304 / *Samuel Johnson, Moralist, 1784*			
Pr		Com. Martyr or Num. 24. 2–7, 15–17 / also Wisd. 3. 1–7 Ps. 25. 3–8 / 2 Cor. 4. 6–15 Matt. 21. 23–27	Ps. 40 / alt. Ps. 44 / Isa. 38. 1–8, 21–22 / Matt. 16. 13–end	Ps. 25; **26** / alt. Ps. **47**; 49 / Isa. 49. 14–25 / 1 Thess. 5. 1–11

* For Ember Day provision, see p. 11.

	Calendar and Holy Communion	Morning Prayer	Evening Prayer	NOTES
	THE SECOND SUNDAY IN ADVENT			
P	2 Kings 22. 8–10; 23. 1–3 Ps. 50. 1–6 Rom. 15. 4–13 Luke 21. 25–33	Ps. 40 Isa. 64. 1–7 Luke 3. 1–6	Ps. 75 [76] Mal. 3. 1–4 Luke 1. 1–25	
	Nicholas, Bishop of Myra, c. 326			
Pw	Com. Bishop	Isa. 30. 1–18 Matt. 14. 1–12	Isa. 45. 14–end 1 Thess. ch. 1	
P		Isa. 30. 19–end Matt. 14. 13–end	Isa. ch. 46 1 Thess. 2. 1–12	
	The Conception of the Blessed Virgin Mary			
Pw		Isa. ch. 31 Matt. 15. 1–20	Isa. ch. 47 1 Thess. 2. 13–end	
P		Isa. ch. 32 Matt. 15. 21–28	Isa. 48. 1–11 1 Thess. ch. 3	
P		Isa. 33. 1–22 Matt. 15. 29–end	Isa. 48. 12–end 1 Thess. 4. 1–12	
P		Isa. ch. 35 Matt. 16. 1–12	Isa. 49. 1–13 1 Thess. 4. 13–end	
			ct	
	THE THIRD SUNDAY IN ADVENT			
P	Isa. ch. 35 Ps. 80. 1–7 1 Cor. 4. 1–5 Matt. 11. 2–10	Ps. 12; 14 Isa. 25. 1–9 Luke 3. 7–18	Ps. 62 Zeph. 3. 14–end Luke 1. 57–66 [67–end]	
	Lucy, Martyr at Syracuse, 304			
Pr	Com. Virgin Martyr	Isa. 38. 1–8, 21–22 Matt. 16. 13–end	Isa. 49. 14–25 1 Thess. 5. 1–11	

		Sunday Principal Service Weekday Eucharist	Third Service Morning Prayer	Second Service Evening Prayer
14 Tuesday	John of the Cross, Poet, Teacher, 1591			
Pw	Com. Teacher *or* *esp.* 1 Cor. 2. 1–10 *also* John 14. 18–23	Zeph. 3. 1–2, 9–13 Ps. 34. 1–6, 21–22 Matt. 21. 28–32	Ps. *70*; 74 *alt.* Ps. *48*; 52 Isa. 38. 9–20 Matt. 17. 1–13	Ps. *50*; 54 *alt.* Ps. 50 Isa. ch. 50 1 Thess. 5. 12–end
15 Wednesday				
P		Isa. 45. 6b–8, 18, 21b–end Ps. 85. 7–end Luke 7. 18b–23	Ps. *75*; 96 *alt.* Ps. 119. 57–80 Isa. ch. 39 Matt. 17. 14–21	Ps. 25; *82* *alt.* Ps. *59*; 60; (67) Isa. 51. 1–8 2 Thess. ch. 1
16 Thursday				
P		Isa. 54. 1–10 Ps. 30. 1–5, 11–end Luke 7. 24–30	Ps. *76*; 97 *alt.* Ps. 56; *57*; (63†) Zeph. 1.1 – 2.3 Matt. 17. 22–end	Ps. 44 *alt.* Ps. 61; *62*; 64 Isa. 51. 9–16 2 Thess. ch. 2
17 Friday	O Sapientia *Eglantyne Jebb, Social Reformer, Founder of 'Save the Children', 1928*			
P		Gen. 49. 2, 8–10 Ps. 72. 1–5, 18–19 Matt. 1. 1–17	Ps. 77; *98* *alt.* Ps. *51*; 54 Zeph. 3. 1–13 Matt. 18. 1–20	Ps. 49 *alt.* Ps. 38 Isa. 51. 17–end 2 Thess. ch. 3
18 Saturday				
P		Jer. 23. 5–8 Ps. 72. 1–2, 12–13, 18–end Matt. 1. 18–24	Ps. 71 *alt.* Ps. 68 Zeph. 3. 14–end Matt. 18. 21–end	Ps. 42; *43* *alt.* Ps. 65; *66* Isa. 52. 1–12 Jude **ct**
19 Sunday	**THE FOURTH SUNDAY OF ADVENT**			
P		Mic. 5. 2–5a *Canticle*: Magnificat *or* Ps. 80. 1–8 Heb. 10. 5–10 Luke 1. 39–45 [46–55]	Ps. 144 Isa. 32. 1–8 Rev. 22. 6–end	Ps. 123; [131] Isa. 10.33 – 11.10 Matt. 1. 18–end
20 Monday				
P		Isa. 7. 10–14 Ps. 24. 1–6 Luke 1. 26–38	Ps. *46*; 95 Mal. 1. 1, 6–end Matt. 19. 1–12	Ps. *4*; 9 Isa. 52.13 – 53.end 1 Pet. 1. 1–15
21 Tuesday*				
P		Zeph. 3. 14–18 Ps. 33. 1–4, 11–12, 20–end Luke 1. 39–45	Ps. *121*; 122; 123 Mal. 2. 1–16 Matt. 19. 13–15	Ps. 80; *84* Isa. ch. 54 2 Pet. 1.16 – 2.3
22 Wednesday				
P		1 Sam. 1. 24–end Ps. 113 Luke 1. 46–56	Ps. *124*; 125; 126; 127 Mal. 2.17 – 3.12 Matt. 19. 16–end	Ps. 24; *48* Isa. ch. 55 2 Pet. 2. 4–end

*Thomas the Apostle may be celebrated on 21 December instead of 3 July.

	Calendar and Holy Communion	Morning Prayer	Evening Prayer	NOTES
P		Isa. 38. 9–20 Matt. 17. 1–13	Isa. ch. 50 1 Thess. 5. 12–end	
	Ember Day			
P	Ember CEG	Isa. ch. 39 Matt. 17. 14–21	Isa. 51. 1–8 2 Thess. ch. 1	
	O Sapientia			
P		Zeph. 1.1 – 2.3 Matt. 17. 22–end	Isa. 51. 9–16 2 Thess. ch. 2	
	Ember Day			
P	Ember CEG	Zeph. 3. 1–13 Matt. 18. 1–20	Isa. 51. 17–end 2 Thess. ch. 3	
	Ember Day			
P	Ember CEG	Zeph. 3. 14–end Matt. 18. 21–end	Isa. 52. 1–12 Jude	
			ct	
	THE FOURTH SUNDAY IN ADVENT			
P	Isa. 40. 1–9 Ps. 145. 17–end Phil. 4. 4–7 John 1. 19–28	Ps. 144 Isa. 32. 1–8 Rev. 22. 6–end	Ps. 123; [131] Isa. 10.33 – 11.10 Matt. 1. 18–end	
P		Mal. 1. 1, 6–end Matt. 19. 1–12	Isa. 52.13 – 53.end 1 Pet. 1. 1–15 *or First EP of Thomas* (Ps. 27) Isa. ch. 35 Heb. 10.35 – 11.1 **R ct**	
	THOMAS THE APOSTLE			
R	Job 42. 1–6 Ps. 139. 1–11 Eph. 2. 19–end John 20. 24–end	(Ps. 92; 146) 2 Sam. 15. 17–21 *or* Ecclus. ch. 2 John 11. 1–16	(Ps. 139) Hab. 2. 1–4 1 Pet. 1. 3–12	
P		Mal. 2.17 – 3.12 Matt. 19. 16–end	Isa. ch. 55 2 Pet. 2. 4–end	

		Sunday Principal Service Weekday Eucharist	Third Service Morning Prayer	Second Service Evening Prayer
23 Thursday				
P		Mal. 3. 1–4; 4. 5–end Ps. 25. 3–9 Luke 1. 57–66	Ps. 128; 129; **130**; 131 Mal. 3.13 – 4.end Matt. 23. 1–12	Ps. 89. 1–37 Isa. 56. 1–8 2 Pet. ch. 3
24 Friday	**CHRISTMAS EVE**			
P		*Morning Eucharist* 2 Sam. 7. 1–5, 8–11, 16 Ps. 89. 2, 19–27 Acts 13. 16–26 Luke 1. 67–79	Ps. 45; 113 Nahum ch. 1 Matt. 23. 13–28	Ps. 85 Zech. ch. 2 Rev. 1. 1–8
25 Saturday	**CHRISTMAS DAY**			
𝔴	*Any of the following sets of readings may be used on the evening of Christmas Eve and on Christmas Day. Set III should be used at some service during the celebration.*	*I* Isa. 9. 2–7 Ps. 96 Titus 2. 11–14 Luke 2. 1–14 [15–20] *II* Isa. 62. 6–end Ps. 97 Titus 3. 4–7 Luke 2. [1–7] 8–20 *III* Isa. 52. 7–10 Ps. 98 Heb. 1. 1–4 [5–12] John 1. 1–14	*MP*: Ps. **110**; 117 Isa. 62. 1–5 Matt. 1. 18–end	*EP*: Ps. 8 Isa. 65. 17–25 Phil. 2. 5–11 *or* Luke 2. 1–20 *if it has not been used at the principal service of the day*
26 Sunday	**STEPHEN, DEACON, FIRST MARTYR** (or transferred to 29 December)			
R	*The reading from Acts must be used as either the first or second reading at the Eucharist.*	2 Chron. 24. 20–22 *or* Acts 7. 51–end Ps. 119. 161–168 Acts 7. 51–end *or* Gal. 2. 16b–20 Matt. 10. 17–22	*MP*: Ps. **13**; 31. 1–8; 150 Jer. 26. 12–15 Acts ch. 6	*EP*: Ps. 57; **86** Gen. 4. 1–10 Matt. 23. 34–end
W	*or, for The First Sunday of Christmas:*	1 Sam. 2. 18–20, 26 Ps. 148 (*or* 148. 7–end) Col. 3. 12–17 Luke 2. 41–end	Ps. 105. 1–11 Isa. 41.21 – 42.1 1 John 1. 1–7	Ps. 132 Isa. ch. 61 Gal. 3.27 – 4.7 *Gospel:* Luke 2. 15–21
27 Monday	**JOHN, APOSTLE AND EVANGELIST**			
W		Exod. 33. 7–11a Ps. 117 1 John ch. 1 John 21. 19b–end	*MP*: Ps. **21**; 147. 13–end Exod. 33. 12–end 1 John 2. 1–11	*EP*: Ps. 97 Isa. 6. 1–8 1 John 5. 1–12

	Calendar and Holy Communion	Morning Prayer	Evening Prayer

P		Mal. 3.13 – 4.end Matt. 23. 1–12	Isa. 56. 1–8 2 Pet. ch. 3

CHRISTMAS EVE

P	Collect (1) Christmas Eve (2) Advent 1 Mic. 5. 2–5a Ps. 24 Titus 3. 3–7 Luke 2. 1–14	Nahum ch. 1 Matt. 23. 13–28	Zech. ch. 2 Rev. 1. 1–8

CHRISTMAS DAY

𝖜	Isa. 9. 2–7 Ps. 98 Heb. 1. 1–12 John 1. 1–14	Ps. 110; 117 Isa. 62. 1–5 Matt. 1. 18–end	Ps. 8 Isa. 65. 17–25 Phil. 2. 5–11 or Luke 2. 1–20

STEPHEN, DEACON, FIRST MARTYR (or transferred to 29 December)

R	Collect (1) Stephen (2) Christmas 2 Chron. 24. 20–22 Ps. 119. 161–168 Acts 7. 55–end Matt. 23. 34–end	Ps. 13; 31. 1–8; 150 Jer. 26. 12–15 Acts ch. 6	Ps. 57; 86 Gen. 4. 1–10 Matt. 10. 17–22
	or, for The Sunday after Christmas Day:		
W	Isa. 62. 10–12 Ps. 45. 1–7 Gal. 4. 1–7 Matt. 1. 18–end	Ps. 105. 1–11 Isa. 41.21 – 42.1 1 John 1. 1–7	Ps. 132 Isa. ch. 61 Luke 2. 15–21

JOHN, APOSTLE AND EVANGELIST

W	Collect (1) John (2) Christmas Exod. 33. 18–end Ps. 92. 11–end 1 John ch. 1 John 21. 19b–end	(Ps. 21; 147. 13–end) Exod. 33. 7–11a 1 John 2. 1–11	(Ps. 97) Isa. 6. 1–8 1 John 5. 1–12

		Sunday Principal Service Weekday Eucharist	Third Service Morning Prayer	Second Service Evening Prayer
28 Tuesday	**THE HOLY INNOCENTS**			
R		Jer. 31. 15–17 Ps. 124 1 Cor. 1. 26–29 Matt. 2. 13–18	*MP*: Ps. ***36***; 146 Baruch 4. 21–27 *or* Gen. 37. 13–20 Matt. 18. 1–10	*EP*: Ps. 123; ***128*** Isa. 49. 14–25 Mark 10. 13–16
29 Wednesday	**Thomas Becket, Archbishop of Canterbury, Martyr, 1170*** (For Stephen, Deacon, First Martyr, see provision on 26 December.)			
Wr	Com. Martyr *or* *esp.* Matt. 10. 28–33 *also* Ecclus. 51. 1–8	1 John 2. 3–11 Ps. 96. 1–4 Luke 2. 22–35	Ps. ***19***; 20 Jonah ch. 1 Col. 1. 1–14	Ps. 131; ***132*** Isa. 57. 15–end John 1. 1–18
30 Thursday				
W		1 John 2. 12–17 Ps. 96. 7–10 Luke 2. 36–40	Ps. 111; 112; ***113*** Jonah ch. 2 Col. 1. 15–23	Ps. ***65***; 84 Isa. 59. 1–15a John 1. 19–28
31 Friday	*John Wyclif, Reformer, 1384*			
W		1 John 2. 18–21 Ps. 96. 1, 11–end John 1. 1–18	Ps. 102 Jonah chs 3 & 4 Col. 1.24 - 2.7	Ps. ***90***; 148 Isa. 59. 15b–end John 1. 29–34 *or First EP of The Naming of Jesus* Ps. 148 Jer. 23. 1–6 Col. 2. 8–15 **ct**

January 2022

1 Saturday	**THE NAMING AND CIRCUMCISION OF JESUS**			
W		Num. 6. 22–end Ps. 8 Gal. 4. 4–7 Luke 2. 15–21	*MP*: Ps. ***103***; 150 Gen. 17. 1–13 Rom. 2. 17–end	*EP*: Ps. 115 Deut. 30. [1–10] 11–end Acts 3. 1–16
2 Sunday	**THE SECOND SUNDAY OF CHRISTMAS** *or* The Epiphany (*see provision on 6 January*)			
W		Jer. 31. 7–14 Ps. 147. 13–end *or* Ecclus. 24. 1–12 *Canticle*: Wisd. 10. 15–end Eph. 1. 3–14 John 1. [1–9] 10–18	Ps. 87 Isa. ch. 12 1 Thess. 2. 1–8	Ps. 135 (*or* 135. 1–14) 1 Sam. 1. 20–end 1 John 4. 7–16 *Gospel*: Matt. 2. 13–end

*Thomas Becket may be celebrated on 7 July instead of 29 December.

	Calendar and Holy Communion	Morning Prayer	Evening Prayer	NOTES
	THE HOLY INNOCENTS			
R	Collect (1) Innocents (2) Christmas Jer. 31. 10–17 Ps. 123 Rev. 14. 1–5 Matt. 2. 13–18	(Ps. *36*; 146) Baruch 4. 21–27 or Gen. 37. 13–20 Matt. 18. 1–10	(Ps. 124; *128*) Isa. 49. 14–25 Mark 10. 13–16	
W	CEG of Christmas	Jonah ch. 1 Col. 1. 1–14	Isa. 57. 15–end John 1. 1–18	
W		Jonah ch. 2 Col. 1. 15–23	Isa. 59. 1–15a John 1. 19–28	
	Silvester, Bishop of Rome, 335			
W	Com. Bishop	Jonah chs 3 & 4 Col. 1.24 – 2.7	Isa. 59. 15b–end John 1. 29–34 or First EP of The Circumcision of Christ (Ps. 148) Jer. 23. 1–6 Col. 2. 8–15	
			ct	
	THE CIRCUMCISION OF CHRIST			
W	Additional collect Gen. 17. 3b–10 Ps. 98 Rom. 4. 8–13 or Eph. 2. 11–18 Luke 2. 15–21	(Ps. 103; 150) Gen. 17. 1–13 Rom. 2. 17–end	(Ps. 115) Deut. 30. [1–10] 11–end Acts 3. 1–16	
	THE SECOND SUNDAY AFTER CHRISTMAS			
W	Exod. 24. 12–18 Ps. 93 2 Cor. 8. 9 John 1. 14–18	Ps. 87 Isa. ch. 12 1 Thess. 2. 1–8	Ps. 135 (or 135. 1–14) 1 Sam. 1. 20–end 1 John 4. 7–16	

		Sunday Principal Service Weekday Eucharist	Third Service Morning Prayer	Second Service Evening Prayer
3 Monday				
	W	1 John 2.29 – 3.6 Ps. 98. 2–7 John 1. 29–34	Ps. **127**; 128; 131 Ruth ch. 2 Col. 3. 1–11	Ps. **2**; 110 Isa. 60. 13–end John 1. 43–end
		or, if The Epiphany is celebrated on 2 January: 1 John 3.22 – 4.6 Ps. 2. 7–end Matt. 4. 12–17, 23–end	Ps. **127**; 128; 131 *alt.* Ps. 71 Ruth ch. 1 Col. 2. 8–end	Ps. **2**; 110 *alt.* Ps. **72**; 75 Isa. 60. 1–12 John 1. 35–42
4 Tuesday				
	W	1 John 3. 7–10 Ps. 98. 1, 8–end John 1. 35–42	Ps. 89. 1–37 Ruth ch. 3 Col. 3.12 – 4.1	Ps. 85; **87** Isa. ch. 61 John 2. 1–12
		or, if The Epiphany is celebrated on 2 January: 1 John 4. 7–10 Ps. 72. 1–8 Mark 6. 34–44	Ps. 89. 1–37 *alt.* Ps. 73 Ruth ch. 2 Col. 3. 1–11	Ps. 85; **87** *alt.* Ps. 74 Isa. 60. 13–end John 1. 43–end
5 Wednesday				
	W	1 John 3. 11–21 Ps. 100 John 1. 43–end	Ps. 8; **48** Ruth 4. 1–17 Col. 4. 2–end	*First EP of The Epiphany* Ps. **96**; 97 Isa. 49. 1–13 John 4. 7–26 **𝔚 ct**
		or, if The Epiphany is celebrated on 2 January: 1 John 4. 11–18 Ps. 72. 1, 10–13 Mark 6. 45–52	Ps. 8; **48** *alt.* Ps. 77 Ruth ch. 3 Col. 3.12 – 4.1	Ps. 45; **46** *alt.* Ps. 119. 81–104 Isa. ch. 61 John 2. 1–12
6 Thursday		**THE EPIPHANY**		
	𝔚	Isa. 60. 1–6 Ps. 72 (*or* 72. 10–15) Eph. 3. 1–12 Matt. 2. 1–12	*MP*: Ps. **132**; 113 Jer. 31. 7–14 John 1. 29–34	*EP*: Ps. **98**; 100 Baruch 4.36 – 5.end *or* Isa. 60. 1–9 John 2. 1–11
	W	*or, if The Epiphany is celebrated on 2 January*: 1 John 4.19 – 5.4 Ps. 72. 1, 17–end Luke 4. 14–22	Ps. 18. 1–30 *alt.* Ps. 78. 1–39† Ruth 4. 1–17 Col. 4. 2–end	Ps. 45; **46** *alt.* Ps. 78. 40–end† Isa. ch. 62 John 2. 13–end
7 Friday				
	W	1 John 3.22 – 4.6 Ps. 2. 7–end Matt. 4. 12–17, 23–end	Ps. **99**; 147. 1–12 *alt.* Ps. 55 Baruch 1.15 – 2.10 *or* Jer. 23. 1–8 Matt. 20. 1–16	Ps. 118 *alt.* Ps. 69 Isa. 63. 7–end 1 John ch. 3
		or, if The Epiphany is celebrated on 2 January: 1 John 5. 5–13 Ps. 147. 13–end Luke 5. 12–16	Ps. **99**; 147. 1–12 *alt.* Ps. 55 Baruch 1.15 – 2.10 *or* Jer. 23. 1–8 Matt. 20. 1–16	Ps. 118 *alt.* Ps. 69 Isa. 63. 7–end 1 John ch. 3

	Calendar and Holy Communion	Morning Prayer	Evening Prayer	NOTES
W		Ruth ch. 2 Col. 3. 1–11	Isa. 60. 13–end John 1. 43–end	
W		Ruth ch. 3 Col. 3.12 – 4.1	Isa. ch. 61 John 2. 1–12	
W		Ruth 4. 1–17 Col. 4. 2–end	*First EP of The Epiphany* Ps. **96**; 97 Isa. 49. 1–13 John 4. 7–26	
			𝔚 ct	

THE EPIPHANY

	Calendar and Holy Communion	Morning Prayer	Evening Prayer	NOTES
𝖜	Isa. 60. 1–9 Ps. 100 Eph. 3. 1–12 Matt. 2. 1–12	Ps. 132; 113 Jer. 31. 7–14 John 1. 29–34	Ps. 72; 98 Baruch 4.36 – 5.end *or* Isa. 60. 1–9 John 2. 1–11	
W *or* **G**		Baruch 1.15 – 2.10 *or* Jer. 23. 1–8 Matt. 20. 1–16	Isa. 63. 7–end 1 John ch. 3	

		Sunday Principal Service Weekday Eucharist	Third Service Morning Prayer	Second Service Evening Prayer
8	Saturday			
W		1 John 4. 7–10 Ps. 72. 1–8 Mark 6. 34–44	Ps. **46**; 147. 13–end *alt.* Ps. **76**; 79 Baruch 2. 11–end *or* Jer. 30. 1–17 Matt. 20. 17–28	*First EP of The Baptism of Christ* Ps. 36 Isa. ch. 61 Titus 2. 11–14; 3. 4–7 𝔚 ct
	or, if The Epiphany is celebrated on 2 January:			
		1 John 5. 14–end Ps. 149. 1–5 John 3. 22–30	Ps. **46**; 147. 13–end *alt.* Ps. **76**; 79 Baruch 2. 11–end *or* Jer. 30. 1–17 Matt. 20. 17–28	*First EP of The Baptism of Christ* Ps. 36 Isa. ch. 61 Titus 2. 11–14; 3. 4–7 𝔚 ct
9	**Sunday**	**THE BAPTISM OF CHRIST (THE FIRST SUNDAY OF EPIPHANY)**		
𝔚		Isa. 43. 1–7 Ps. 29 Acts 8. 14–17 Luke 3. 15–17, 21–22	Ps. 89. 19–29 Isa. 42. 1–9 Acts 19. 1–7	Ps. 46; 47 Isa. 55. 1–11 Rom. 6. 1–11 *Gospel:* Mark 1. 4–11
10	Monday	*William Laud, Archbishop of Canterbury, 1645*		
W **DEL 1**		1 Sam. 1. 1–8 Ps. 116. 10–15 Mark 1. 14–20	Ps. **2**; 110 *alt.* Ps. **80**; 82 Gen. 1. 1–19 Matt. 21. 1–17	Ps. **34**; 36 *alt.* Ps. **85**; 86 Amos ch. 1 1 Cor. 1. 1–17
11	Tuesday	*Mary Slessor, Missionary in West Africa, 1915*		
W		1 Sam. 1. 9–20 *Canticle:* 1 Sam. 2. 1, 4–8 *or* Magnificat Mark 1. 21–28	Ps. 8; **9** *alt.* Ps. 87; **89. 1–18** Gen. 1.20 – 2.3 Matt. 21. 18–32	Ps. **45**; 46 *alt.* Ps. 89. 19–end Amos ch. 2 1 Cor. 1. 18–end
12	Wednesday	*Aelred of Hexham, Abbot of Rievaulx, 1167* *Benedict Biscop, Abbot of Wearmouth, Scholar, 689*		
W		Com. Religious *or* *also* Ecclus. 15. 1–6	1 Sam. 3. 1–10, 19–20 Ps. 40. 1–4, 7–10 Mark 1. 29–39	Ps. 19; **20** *alt.* Ps. 119. 105–128 Gen. 2. 4–end Matt. 21. 33–end	Ps. **47**; 48 *alt.* Ps. **91**; 93 Amos ch. 3 1 Cor. ch. 2
13	Thursday	*Hilary, Bishop of Poitiers, Teacher, 367* *Kentigern (Mungo), Missionary Bishop in Strathclyde and Cumbria, 603; George Fox, Founder of the Society of Friends (the Quakers), 1691*		
W		Com. Teacher *or* *also* 1 John 2. 18–25 John 8. 25–32	1 Sam. 4. 1–11 Ps. 44. 10–15, 24–25 Mark 1. 40–end	Ps. **21**; 24 *alt.* Ps. 90; **92** Gen. ch. 3 Matt. 22. 1–14	Ps. **61**; 65 *alt.* Ps. 94 Amos ch. 4 1 Cor. ch. 3
14	Friday			
W		1 Sam. 8. 4–7, 10–end Ps. 89. 15–18 Mark 2. 1–12	Ps. **67**; 72 *alt.* Ps. **88**; (95) Gen. 4. 1–16, 25–26 Matt. 22. 15–33	Ps. 68 *alt.* Ps. 102 Amos 5. 1–17 1 Cor. ch. 4

	Calendar and Holy Communion	Morning Prayer	Evening Prayer	NOTES
	Lucian, Priest and Martyr, 290			
Wr or **Gr**	Com. Martyr	Baruch 2. 11–end or Jer. 30. 1–17 Matt. 20. 17–28	Isa. ch. 64 1 John 4. 7–end	
		ct		
	THE FIRST SUNDAY AFTER THE EPIPHANY To celebrate The Baptism of Christ, see *Common Worship* provision.			
W or **G**	Zech. 8. 1–8 Ps. 72. 1–8 Rom. 12. 1–5 Luke 2. 41–end	Ps. 89. 19–29 Isa. 42. 1–9 Acts 19. 1–7	Ps. 46; 47 Isa. 55. 1–11 Rom. 6. 1–11	
W or **G**		Gen. 1. 1–19 Matt. 21. 1–17	Amos ch. 1 1 Cor. 1. 1–17	
W or **G**		Gen. 1.20 – 2.3 Matt. 21. 18–32	Amos ch. 2 1 Cor. 1. 18–end	
W or **G**		Gen. 2. 4–end Matt. 21. 33–end	Amos ch. 3 1 Cor. ch. 2	
	Hilary, Bishop of Poitiers, Teacher, 367			
W or **Gw**	Com. Doctor	Gen. ch. 3 Matt. 22. 1–14	Amos ch. 4 1 Cor. ch. 3	
W or **G**		Gen. 4. 1–16, 25–26 Matt. 22. 15–33	Amos 5. 1–17 1 Cor. ch. 4	

		Sunday Principal Service Weekday Eucharist	Third Service Morning Prayer	Second Service Evening Prayer
15 Saturday				
W		1 Sam. 9. 1–4, 17–19; 10. 1a Ps. 21. 1–6 Mark 2. 13–17	Ps. 29; *33* *alt.* Ps. 96; *97*; 100 Gen. 6. 1–10 Matt. 22. 34–end	Ps. 84; *85* *alt.* Ps. 104 Amos 5. 18–end 1 Cor. ch. 5 **ct**
16 Sunday	**THE SECOND SUNDAY OF EPIPHANY**			
W		Isa. 62. 1–5 Ps. 36. 5–10 1 Cor. 12. 1–11 John 2. 1–11	Ps. 145. 1–13 Isa. 49. 1–7 Acts 16. 11–15	Ps. 96 1 Sam. 3. 1–20 Eph. 4. 1–16 *Gospel:* John 1. 29–42
17 Monday	**Antony of Egypt, Hermit, Abbot, 356** *Charles Gore, Bishop, Founder of the Community of the Resurrection, 1932*			
W **DEL 2**	Com. Religious *or* *esp.* Phil. 3. 7–14 *also* Matt. 19. 16–26	1 Sam. 15. 16–23 Ps. 50. 8–10, 16–17, 24 Mark 2. 18–22	Ps. 145; *146* *alt.* Ps. **98**; 99; 101 Gen. 6.11 – 7.10 Matt. 24. 1–14	Ps. 71 *alt.* Ps. 105† (*or* Ps. 103) Amos ch. 6 1 Cor. 6. 1–11
18 Tuesday	*Amy Carmichael, Founder of the Dohnavur Fellowship, Spiritual Writer, 1951* *The Week of Prayer for Christian Unity until 25 January*			
W		1 Sam. 16. 1–13 Ps. 89. 19–27 Mark 2. 23–end	Ps. *132*; 147. 1–12 *alt.* Ps. 106† (*or* Ps. 103) Gen. 7. 11–end Matt. 24. 15–28	Ps. 89. 1–37 *alt.* Ps. 107† Amos ch. 7 1 Cor. 6. 12–end
19 Wednesday	**Wulfstan, Bishop of Worcester, 1095**			
W	Com. Bishop *or* *esp.* Matt. 24. 42–46	1 Sam. 17. 32–33, 37, 40–51 Ps. 144. 1–2, 9–10 Mark 3. 1–6	Ps. *81*; 147. 13–end *alt.* Ps. 110; *111*; 112 Gen. 8. 1–14 Matt. 24. 29–end	Ps. *97*; 98 *alt.* Ps. 119. 129–152 Amos ch. 8 1 Cor. 7. 1–24
20 Thursday	*Richard Rolle of Hampole, Spiritual Writer, 1349*			
W		1 Sam. 18. 6–9; 19. 1–7 Ps. 56. 1–2, 8–end Mark 3. 7–12	Ps. *76*; 148 *alt.* Ps. 113; *115* Gen. 8.15 – 9.7 Matt. 25. 1–13	Ps. 99; 100; *111* *alt.* Ps. 114; *116*; 117 Amos ch. 9 1 Cor. 7. 25–end
21 Friday	**Agnes, Child Martyr at Rome, 304**			
Wr	Com. Martyr *or* *also* Rev. 7. 13–end	1 Sam. 24. 3–22a Ps. 57. 1–2, 8–end Mark 3. 13–19	Ps. *27*; 149 *alt.* Ps. 139 Gen. 9. 8–19 Matt. 25. 14–30	Ps. 73 *alt.* Ps. *130*; 131; 137 Hos. 1.1 – 2.1 1 Cor. ch. 8
22 Saturday	*Vincent of Saragossa, Deacon, first Martyr of Spain, 304*			
W		2 Sam. 1. 1–4, 11–12, 17–19, 23–end Ps. 80. 1–6 Mark 3. 20–21	Ps. *122*; 128; 150 *alt.* Ps. 120; *121*; 122 Gen. 11. 1–9 Matt. 25. 31–end	Ps. *61*; 66 *alt.* Ps. 118 Hos. 2. 2–17 1 Cor. 9. 1–14 **ct**
23 Sunday	**THE THIRD SUNDAY OF EPIPHANY**			
W		Neh. 8. 1–3, 5–6, 8–10 Ps. 19 (*or* 19. 1–6) 1 Cor. 12. 12–31a Luke 4. 14–21	Ps. 113 Deut. 30. 11–15 3 John 1, 5–8	Ps. 33 (*or* 33. 1–12) Num. 9. 15–end 1 Cor. 7. 17–24 *Gospel:* Mark 1. 21–28

	Calendar and Holy Communion	Morning Prayer	Evening Prayer	NOTES
W or **G**		Gen. 6. 1–10 Matt. 22. 34–end	Amos 5. 18–end 1 Cor. ch. 5	
			ct	

THE SECOND SUNDAY AFTER THE EPIPHANY

	Calendar and Holy Communion	Morning Prayer	Evening Prayer	NOTES
W or **G**	2 Kings 4. 1–17 Ps. 107. 13–22 Rom. 12. 6–16a John 2. 1–11	Ps. 145. 1–13 Isa. 49. 1–7 Acts 16. 11–15	Ps. 96 1 Sam. 3. 1–20 Eph. 4. 1–16	
W or **G**		Gen. 6.11 – 7.10 Matt. 24. 1–14	Amos ch. 6 1 Cor. 6. 1–11	

Prisca, Martyr at Rome, c. 265
For the Week of Prayer for Christian Unity, see *Common Worship* provision.

	Calendar and Holy Communion	Morning Prayer	Evening Prayer	NOTES
Wr or **Gr**	Com. Virgin Martyr	Gen. 7. 11–end Matt. 24. 15–28	Amos ch. 7 1 Cor. 6. 12–end	
W or **G**		Gen. 8. 1–14 Matt. 24. 29–end	Amos ch. 8 1 Cor. 7. 1–24	

Fabian, Bishop of Rome, Martyr, 250

	Calendar and Holy Communion	Morning Prayer	Evening Prayer	NOTES
Wr or **Gr**	Com. Martyr	Gen. 8.15 – 9.7 Matt. 25. 1–13	Amos ch. 9 1 Cor. 7. 25–end	

Agnes, Child Martyr at Rome, 304

	Calendar and Holy Communion	Morning Prayer	Evening Prayer	NOTES
Wr or **Gr**	Com. Virgin Martyr	Gen. 9. 8–19 Matt. 25. 14–30	Hos. 1.1 – 2.1 1 Cor. ch. 8	

Vincent of Saragossa, Deacon, first Martyr of Spain, 304

	Calendar and Holy Communion	Morning Prayer	Evening Prayer	NOTES
Wr or **Gr**	Com. Martyr	Gen. 11. 1–9 Matt. 25. 31–end	Hos. 2. 2–17 1 Cor. 9. 1–14	
			ct	

THE THIRD SUNDAY AFTER THE EPIPHANY

	Calendar and Holy Communion	Morning Prayer	Evening Prayer	NOTES
W or **G**	2 Kings 6. 14b–23 Ps. 102. 15–22 Rom. 12. 16b–end Matt. 8. 1–13	Ps. 113 Deut. 30. 11–15 3 John 1, 5–8	Ps. 33 (or 33. 1–12) Num. 9. 15–end 1 Cor. 7. 17–24	

		Sunday Principal Service Weekday Eucharist	Third Service Morning Prayer	Second Service Evening Prayer
24 Monday				

Francis de Sales, Bishop of Geneva, Teacher, 1622

		Sunday Principal Service Weekday Eucharist	Third Service Morning Prayer	Second Service Evening Prayer
W **DEL 3**	Com. Teacher *or* *also* Prov. 3. 13–18 John 3. 17–21	2 Sam. 5. 1–7, 10 Ps. 89. 19–27 Mark 3. 22–30	Ps. 40; **108** *alt.* Ps. 123; 124; 125; **126** Gen. 11.27 – 12.9 Matt. 26. 1–16	Ps. **138**; 144 *alt.* Ps. **127**; 128; 129 Hos. 2.18 – 3.end 1 Cor. 9. 15–end *or First EP of The* *Conversion of Paul* Ps. 149 Isa. 49. 1–13 Acts 22. 3–16 **ct**
25 Tuesday	**THE CONVERSION OF PAUL**			
W		Jer. 1. 4–10 *or* Acts 9. 1–22 Ps. 67 Acts 9. 1–22 *or* Gal. 1. 11–16a Matt. 19. 27–end	*MP*: Ps. 66; 147. 13–end Ezek. 3. 22–end Phil. 3. 1–14	*EP*: Ps. 119. 41–56 Ecclus. 39. 1–10 *or* Isa. 56. 1–8 Col. 1.24 – 2.7
26 Wednesday	Timothy and Titus, Companions of Paul			
W	Isa. 61. 1–3a *or* Ps. 100 2 Tim. 2. 1–8 *or* Titus 1. 1–5 Luke 10. 1–9	2 Sam. 7. 4–17 Ps. 89. 19–27 Mark 4. 1–20	Ps. 45; **46** *alt.* Ps. 119. 153–end Gen. ch. 14 Matt. 26. 36–46	Ps. 21; **29** *alt.* Ps. 136 Hos. 5. 1–7 1 Cor. 10.14 – 11.1
27 Thursday				
W		2 Sam. 7. 18–19, 24–end Ps. 132. 1–5, 11–15 Mark 4. 21–25	Ps. **47**; 48 *alt.* Ps. **143**; 146 Gen. ch. 15 Matt. 26. 47–56	Ps. **24**; 33 *alt.* Ps. **138**; 140; 141 Hos. 5.8 – 6.6 1 Cor. 11. 2–16
28 Friday	Thomas Aquinas, Priest, Philosopher, Teacher, 1274			
W	Com. Teacher *or* *esp.* Wisd. 7. 7–10, 15–16 1 Cor. 2. 9–end John 16. 12–15	2 Sam. 11. 1–10, 13–17 Ps. 51. 1–6, 9 Mark 4. 26–34	Ps. 61; **65** *alt.* Ps. 142; **144** Gen. ch. 16 Matt. 26. 57–end	Ps. **67**; 77 *alt.* Ps. **145** Hos. 6.7 – 7.2 1 Cor. 11. 17–end
29 Saturday				
W		2 Sam. 12. 1–7, 10–17 Ps. 51. 11–16 Mark 4. 35–end	Ps. 68 *alt.* Ps. 147 Gen. 17. 1–22 Matt. 27. 1–10	Ps. **72**; 76 *alt.* Ps. **148**; 149; 150 Hos. ch. 8 1 Cor. 12. 1–11 **ct**
30 Sunday	**THE FOURTH SUNDAY OF EPIPHANY** *or The Presentation of Christ in the Temple (Candlemas)**			
W		Ezek. 43.27 – 44.4 Ps. 48 1 Cor. ch. 13 Luke 2. 22–40	Ps. 71. 1–6, 15–17 Mic. 6. 1–8 1 Cor. 6. 12–end	Ps. 34 (*or* 34. 1–10) 1 Chron. 29. 6–19 Acts 7. 44–50 *Gospel*: John 4. 19–29a

*See provision for First EP on 1 February and throughout the day for The Presentation on 2 February.

	Calendar and Holy Communion	Morning Prayer	Evening Prayer	NOTES
W or G		Gen. 11.27 – 12.9 Matt. 26. 1–16	Hos. 2.18 – 3.end 1 Cor. 9. 15-end *or First EP of The Conversion of Paul* (Ps. 149) Isa. 49. 1–13 Acts 22. 3–16	
			W ct	

THE CONVERSION OF PAUL

	Calendar and Holy Communion	Morning Prayer	Evening Prayer	NOTES
W	Josh. 5. 13-end Ps. 67 Acts 9. 1–22 Matt. 19. 27–end	(Ps. 66; 147. 13-end) Ezek. 3. 22-end Phil. 3. 1–14	(Ps. 119. 41–56) Ecclus. 39. 1–10 *or* Isa. 56. 1–8 Col. 1.24 – 2.7	
W or G		Gen. ch. 14 Matt. 26. 36–46	Hos. 5. 1–7 1 Cor. 10.14 – 11.1	
W or G		Gen. ch. 15 Matt. 26. 47–56	Hos. 5.8 – 6.6 1 Cor. 11. 2–16	
W or G		Gen. ch. 16 Matt. 26. 57–end	Hos. 6.7 – 7.2 1 Cor. 11. 17–end	
W or G		Gen. 17. 1–22 Matt. 27. 1–10	Hos. ch. 8 1 Cor. 12. 1–11	
			ct	

THE FOURTH SUNDAY AFTER THE EPIPHANY

	Calendar and Holy Communion	Morning Prayer	Evening Prayer	NOTES
W or G	1 Sam. 10. 17–24 Ps. 97 Rom. 13. 1–7 Matt. 8. 23–34	Ps. 71. 1–6, 15–17 Mic. 6. 1–8 1 Cor. 6. 12–end	Ps. 34 (*or* 34. 1–10) 1 Chron. 29. 6–19 Acts 7. 44–50	

		Sunday Principal Service Weekday Eucharist	Third Service Morning Prayer	Second Service Evening Prayer
31 Monday	*John Bosco, Priest, Founder of the Salesian Teaching Order, 1888* (Ordinary time resumes today if The Presentation is observed on 30 January.)			
W *or* **G** **DEL 4**		2 Sam. 15. 13–14, 30; 16. 5–13 Ps. 3 Mark 5. 1–20	Ps. ***57***; 96 *alt.* Ps. ***1***; 2; 3* Gen. 18. 1–15 Matt. 27. 11–26	Ps. 2; ***20*** *alt.* Ps. ***4***; 7 Hos. ch. 9 1 Cor. 12. 12–end

February 2022

		Sunday Principal Service Weekday Eucharist	Third Service Morning Prayer	Second Service Evening Prayer
1 Tuesday	*Brigid, Abbess of Kildare, c. 525*			
W *or* **G**		2 Sam. 18.9–10, 14, 24–25, 30 – 19.3 Ps. 86. 1–6 Mark. 5. 21–end	Ps. ***93***; 97 *alt.* Ps. ***5***; 6; (8)* Gen. 18. 16–end Matt. 27. 27–44	*First EP of The Presentation* Ps. 118 1 Sam. 1. 19b–end Heb. 4. 11–end **𝔚 ct** *or, if The Presentation is kept on 30 January*: Ps. ***9***; 10† Hos. ch. 10 1 Cor. ch. 13
2 Wednesday	**THE PRESENTATION OF CHRIST IN THE TEMPLE (CANDLEMAS)**			
𝔚		Mal. 3. 1–5 Ps. 24 (*or* 24. 7–end) Heb. 2. 14–end Luke 2. 22–40	*MP*: Ps. ***48***; 146 Exod. 13. 1–16 Rom. 12. 1–5	*EP*: Ps. 122; ***132*** Hag. 2. 1–9 John 2. 18–22
	or, if The Presentation is observed on 30 January:			
G		2 Sam. 24. 2, 9–17 Ps. 32. 1–8 Mark 6. 1–6a	Ps. 119. 1–32 Gen. 19. 1–3, 12–29 Matt. 27. 45–56	Ps. ***11***; 12; 13 Hos. 11. 1–11 1 Cor. 14. 1–19
3 Thursday	**Anskar, Archbishop of Hamburg, Missionary in Denmark and Sweden, 865** Ordinary Time starts today (or on 31 January if The Presentation is observed on 30 January)			
Gw	Com. Missionary *or* *esp.* Isa. 52. 7–10 *also* Rom. 10. 11–15	1 Kings 2. 1–4, 10–12 *Canticle*: 1 Chron. 29. 10–12 *or* Ps. 145. 1–5 Mark 6. 7–13	Ps. 14; ***15***; 16 Gen. 21. 1–21 Matt. 27. 57–end	Ps. 18 Hos. 11.12 – 12.end 1 Cor. 14. 20–end
4 Friday	*Gilbert of Sempringham, Founder of the Gilbertine Order, 1189*			
G		Ecclus. 47. 2–11 Ps. 18. 31–36, 50–end Mark 6. 14–29	Ps. 17; ***19*** Gen. 22. 1–19 Matt. 28. 1–15	Ps. 22 Hos. 13. 1–14 1 Cor. 16. 1–9
5 Saturday				
G		1 Kings 3. 4–13 Ps. 119. 9–16 Mark 6. 30–34	Ps. 20; 21; ***23*** Gen. ch. 23 Matt. 28. 16–end	Ps. ***24***; 25 Hos. ch. 14 1 Cor. 16. 10–end **ct**
6 Sunday	**THE FOURTH SUNDAY BEFORE LENT (Proper 1)** (The Accession of Queen Elizabeth II may be observed on 6 February, and Collect, Readings and Post-Communion for the sovereign used.)			
G		Isa. 6. 1–8 [9–end] Ps. 138 1 Cor. 15. 1–111 Luke 5. 1–11	Ps. 3; 4 Jer. 26. 1–16 Acts 3. 1–10	Ps. [1]; 2 Wisd. 6. 1–21 *or* Hos. ch. 1 Col. 3. 1–22 *Gospel*: Matt. 5. 13–20

*If The Presentation was observed on 30 January, the alternative psalms are used.

	Calendar and Holy Communion	Morning Prayer	Evening Prayer	NOTES
W or **G**		Gen. 18. 1–15 Matt. 27. 11–26	Hos. ch. 9 1 Cor. 12. 12–end	
W or **G**		Gen. 18. 16–end Matt. 27. 27–44	*First EP of The Presentation* Ps. 118 1 Sam. 1. 19b–end Heb. 4. 11–end	

𝔚 ct

THE PRESENTATION OF CHRIST IN THE TEMPLE

𝔴	Mal. 3. 1–5 Ps. 48. 1–7 Gal. 4. 1–7 Luke 2. 22–40	Ps. 48; 146 Exod. 13. 1–16 Rom. 12. 1–5	Ps. 122; 132 Hag. 2. 1–9 John 2. 18–22	

Blasius, Bishop of Sebastopol, Martyr, c. 316

Gr	Com. Martyr	Gen. 21. 1–21 Matt. 27. 57–end	Hos. 11.12 – 12.end 1 Cor. 14. 20–end	
G		Gen. 22. 1–19 Matt. 28. 1–15	Hos. 13. 1–14 1 Cor. 16. 1–9	

Agatha, Martyr in Sicily, 251

Gr	Com. Virgin Martyr	Gen. ch. 23 Matt. 28. 16–end	Hos. ch. 14 1 Cor. 16. 10–end	

ct

THE FIFTH SUNDAY AFTER THE EPIPHANY
The Accession of Queen Elizabeth II, 1952

G	Hos. 6. 4–6 Ps. 118. 14–21 Col. 3. 12–17 Matt. 13. 24b–30	Ps. 3; 4 Jer. 26. 1–16 Acts 3. 1–10	Ps. [1]; 2 Wisd. 6. 1–21 or Hos. ch. 1 Col. 3. 1–22	

	Sunday Principal Service / Weekday Eucharist	Third Service / Morning Prayer	Second Service / Evening Prayer
7 Monday			
G **DEL 5**	1 Kings 8. 1–7, 9–13 Ps. 132. 1–9 Mark 6. 53–end	Ps. 27; **30** Lev. 19. 1–18, 30–end 1 Tim. 1. 1–17	Ps. 26; **28**; 29 1 Chron. 28. 1–10 John 15. 1–11
8 Tuesday			
G	1 Kings 8. 22–23, 27–30 Ps. 84. 1–10 Mark 7. 1–13	Ps. 32; **36** Lev. 23. 1–22 1 Tim. 1.18 – 2.end	Ps. 33 1 Chron. 28. 11–end John 15. 12–17
9 Wednesday			
G	1 Kings 10. 1–10 Ps. 37. 3–6, 30–32 Mark 7. 14–23	Ps. 34 Lev. 23. 23–end 1 Tim. ch. 3	Ps. 119. 33–56 1 Chron. 29. 1–9 John 15. 18–end
10 Thursday	*Scholastica, sister of Benedict, Abbess of Plombariola, c. 543*		
G	1 Kings 11. 4–13 Ps. 106. 3, 35–41 Mark 7. 24–30	Ps. 37† Lev. 24. 1–9 1 Tim. ch. 4	Ps. 39; **40** 1 Chron. 29. 10–20 John 16. 1–15
11 Friday			
G	1 Kings 11. 29–32; 12. 19 Ps. 81. 8–14 Mark 7. 31–end	Ps. 31 Lev. 25. 1–24 1 Tim. 5. 1–16	Ps. 35 1 Chron. 29. 21–end John 16. 16–22
12 Saturday			
G	1 Kings 12. 26–32; 13. 33–end Ps. 106. 6–7, 20–23 Mark 8. 1–10	Ps. 41; **42**; 43 Num. 6. 1–5, 21–end 1 Tim. 5. 17–end	Ps. 45; **46** 2 Chron. 1. 1–13 John 16. 23–end **ct**
13 Sunday	**THE THIRD SUNDAY BEFORE LENT (Proper 2)**		
G	Jer. 17. 5–10 Ps. 1 1 Cor. 15. 12–20 Luke 6. 17–26	Ps. 7 Jer. 30. 1–3, 10–22 Acts ch. 6	Ps. [5]; 6 Wisd. 11.21 – 12.11 *or* Hos. 10. 1–8, 12 Gal. 4. 8–20 *Gospel*: Matt. 5. 21–37
14 Monday	**Cyril and Methodius, Missionaries to the Slavs, 869 and 885** *Valentine, Martyr at Rome, c. 269*		
Gw **DEL 6**	Com. Missionaries *or* *esp.* Isa. 52. 7–10 *also* Rom. 10. 11–15 Jas. 1. 1–11 Ps. 119. 65–72 Mark 8. 11–13	Ps. 44 Gen. 24. 1–28 1 Tim. 6. 1–10	Ps. **47**; 49 2 Chron. 2. 1–16 John 17. 1–5
15 Tuesday	*Sigfrid, Bishop, Apostle of Sweden, 1045; Thomas Bray, Priest, Founder of the SPCK and SPG, 1730*		
G	Jas. 1. 12–18 Ps. 94. 12–18 Mark 8. 14–21	Ps. **48**; 52 Gen. 24. 29–end 1 Tim. 6. 11–end	Ps. 50 2 Chron. ch. 3 John 17. 6–19
16 Wednesday			
G	Jas. 1. 19–end Ps. 15 Mark 8. 22–26	Ps. 119. 57–80 Gen. 25. 7–11, 19–end 2 Tim. 1. 1–14	Ps. **59**; 60; (67) 2 Chron. ch. 5 John 17. 20–end

	Calendar and Holy Communion	Morning Prayer	Evening Prayer	NOTES
G		Lev. 19. 1–18, 30–end 1 Tim. 1. 1–17	1 Chron. 28. 1–10 John 15. 1–11	
G		Lev. 23. 1–22 1 Tim. 1.18 – 2.end	1 Chron. 28. 11–end John 15. 12–17	
G		Lev. 23. 23–end 1 Tim. ch. 3	1 Chron. 29. 1–9 John 15. 18–end	
G		Lev. 24. 1–9 1 Tim. ch. 4	1 Chron. 29. 10–20 John 16. 1–15	
G		Lev. 25. 1–24 1 Tim. 5. 1–16	1 Chron. 29. 21–end John 16. 16–22	
G		Num. 6. 1–5, 21–end 1 Tim. 5. 17–end	2 Chron. 1. 1–13 John 16. 23–end **ct**	

SEPTUAGESIMA

| G | Gen. 1. 1–5
Ps. 9. 10–20
1 Cor. 9. 24–end
Matt. 20. 1–16 | Ps. 7
Jer. 30. 1–3, 10–22
Acts ch. 6 | Ps. [5]; 6
Wisd. 11.21 – 12.11
or Hos. 10. 1–8, 12
Gal. 4. 8–20 | |

Valentine, Martyr at Rome, c. 269

Gr	Com. Martyr	Gen. 24. 1–28 1 Tim. 6. 1–10	2 Chron. 2. 1–16 John 17. 1–5	
G		Gen. 24. 29–end 1 Tim. 6. 11–end	2 Chron. ch. 3 John 17. 6–19	
G		Gen. 25. 7–11, 19–end 2 Tim. 1. 1–14	2 Chron. ch. 5 John 17. 20–end	

		Sunday Principal Service Weekday Eucharist	Third Service Morning Prayer	Second Service Evening Prayer
17 Thursday	Janani Luwum, Archbishop of Uganda, Martyr, 1977			
Gr	Com. Martyr *or* *also* Ecclus. 4. 20–28 John 12. 24–32	Jas. 2. 1–9 Ps. 34. 1–7 Mark 8. 27–33	Ps. 56; **57**; (63†) Gen. 26.34 – 27.40 2 Tim. 1.15 – 2.13	Ps. 61; **62**; 64 2 Chron. 6. 1–21 John 18. 1–11
18 Friday				
G		Jas. 2. 14–24, 26 Ps. 112 Mark 8.34 – 9.1	Ps. **51**; 54 Gen. 27.41 – 28.end 2 Tim. 2. 14–end	Ps. 38 2 Chron. 6. 22–end John 18. 12–27
19 Saturday				
G		Jas. 3. 1–10 Ps. 12. 1–7 Mark 9. 2–13	Ps. 68 Gen. 29. 1–30 2 Tim. ch. 3	Ps. 65; **66** 2 Chron. ch. 7 John 18. 28–end **ct**
20 Sunday	**THE SECOND SUNDAY BEFORE LENT**			
G		Gen. 2. 4b–9, 15–end Ps. 65 Rev. ch. 4 Luke 8. 22–25	Ps. 104. 1–26 Job 28. 1–11 Acts 14. 8–17	Ps. 147 (or 147. 13–end) Gen. 1.1 – 2.3 Matt. 6. 25–end
21 Monday				
G **DEL 7**		Jas. 3. 13–end Ps. 19. 7–end Mark 9. 14–29	Ps. 71 Gen. 29.31 – 30.24 2 Tim. 4. 1–8	Ps. **72**; 75 2 Chron. 9. 1–12 John 19. 1–16
22 Tuesday				
G		Jas. 4. 1–10 Ps. 55. 7–9, 24 Mark 9. 30–37	Ps. 73 Gen. 31. 1–24 2 Tim. 4. 9–end	Ps. 74 2 Chron. 10.1 – 11.4 John 19. 17–30
23 Wednesday	Polycarp, Bishop of Smyrna, Martyr, c. 155			
Gr	Com. Martyr *or* *also* Rev. 2. 8–11	Jas. 4. 13–end Ps. 49. 1–2, 5–10 Mark 9. 38–40	Ps. 77 Gen. 31.25 – 32.2 Titus ch. 1	Ps. 119. 81–104 2 Chron. ch. 12 John 19. 31–end
24 Thursday*				
G		Jas. 5. 1–6 Ps. 49. 12–20 Mark 9. 41–end	Ps. 78. 1–39† Gen. 32. 3–30 Titus ch. 2	Ps. 78. 40–end† 2 Chron. 13.1 – 14.1 John 20. 1–10
25 Friday				
G		Jas. 5. 9–12 Ps. 103. 1–4, 8–13 Mark 10. 1–12	Ps. 55 Gen. 33. 1–17 Titus ch. 3	Ps. 69 2 Chron. 14. 2–end John 20. 11–18
26 Saturday				
G		Jas. 5. 13–end Ps. 141. 1–4 Mark 10. 13–16	Ps. **76**; 79 Gen. ch. 35 Philem.	Ps. 81; **84** 2 Chron. 15. 1–15 John 20. 19–end **ct**

*Matthias may be celebrated on 24 February instead of 14 May.

	Calendar and Holy Communion	Morning Prayer	Evening Prayer	NOTES
G		Gen. 26.34 – 27.40 2 Tim. 1.15 – 2.13	2 Chron. 6. 1–21 John 18. 1–11	
G		Gen. 27.41 – 28.end 2 Tim. 2. 14–end	2 Chron. 6. 22–end John 18. 12–27	
G		Gen. 29. 1–30 2 Tim. ch. 3	2 Chron. ch. 7 John 18. 28–end ct	
	SEXAGESIMA			
G	Gen. 3. 9–19 Ps. 83. 1–2, 13–end 2 Cor. 11. 19–31 Luke 8. 4–15	Ps. 104. 1–26 Job 28. 1–11 Acts 14. 8–17	Ps. 147 (or 147. 13–end) Gen. 1.1 – 2.3 Matt. 6. 25–end	
G		Gen. 29.31 – 30.24 2 Tim. 4. 1–8	2 Chron. 9. 1–12 John 19. 1–16	
G		Gen. 31. 1–24 2 Tim. 4. 9–end	2 Chron. 10.1 – 11.4 John 19. 17–30	
G		Gen. 31.25 – 32.2 Titus ch. 1	2 Chron. ch. 12 John 19. 31–end or First EP of Matthias (Ps. 147) Isa. 22. 15–22 Phil. 3.13b – 4.1 **R** ct	
	MATTHIAS THE APOSTLE			
R	1 Sam. 2. 27–35 Ps. 16. 1–7 Acts 1. 15–end Matt. 1. 25–end	(Ps. 15) Jonah 1. 1–9 Acts 2. 37–end	(Ps. 80) 1 Sam. 16. 1–13a Matt. 7. 15–27	
G		Gen. 33. 1–17 Titus ch. 3	2 Chron. 14. 2–end John 20. 11–18	
G		Gen. ch. 35 Philem.	2 Chron. 15. 1–15 John 20. 19–end ct	

		Sunday Principal Service Weekday Eucharist	Third Service Morning Prayer	Second Service Evening Prayer

27 Sunday   THE SUNDAY NEXT BEFORE LENT

G		Exod. 34. 29–end Ps. 99 2 Cor. 3.12 – 4.2 Luke 9. 28–36 [37–43a]	Ps. 2 Exod. 33. 17–end 1 John 3. 1–3	Ps. 89. 1–18 (*or* 89. 5–12) Exod. 3. 1–6 John 12. 27–36a

28 Monday

G DEL 8		1 Pet. 1. 3–9 Ps. 111 Mark 10. 17–27	*80*; 82 Gen. 37. 1–11 Gal. ch. 1	Ps. *85*; 86 Jer. ch. 1 John 3. 1–21

March 2022

1 Tuesday   David, Bishop of Menevia, Patron of Wales, *c.* 601

Gw		Com. Bishop *or* *also* 2 Sam. 23. 1–4 Ps. 89. 19–22, 24	1 Pet. 1. 10–16 Ps. 98. 1–5 Mark 10. 28–31	Ps. 87; *89. 1–18* Gen. 37. 12–end Gal. 2. 1–10	Ps. 89. 19–end Jer. 2. 1–13 John 3. 22–end

2 Wednesday ASH WEDNESDAY

P		Joel 2. 1–2, 12–17 *or* Isa. 58. 1–12 Ps. 51. 1–18 2 Cor. 5.20b – 6.10 Matt. 6. 1–6, 16–21 *or* John 8. 1–11	*MP*: Ps. 38 Dan. 9. 3–6, 17–19 1 Tim. 6. 6–19	*EP*: Ps. *51 or* Ps. 102 (*or* 102. 1–18) Isa. 1. 10–18 Luke 15. 11–end

3 Thursday

P		Deut. 30. 15–end Ps. 1 Luke 9. 22–25	Ps. 77 *alt.* Ps. 90; *92* Gen. ch. 39 Gal. 2. 11–end	Ps. 74 *alt.* Ps. 94 Jer. 2. 14–32 John 4. 1–26

4 Friday

P		Isa. 58. 1–9a Ps. 51. 1–5, 17–18 Matt. 9. 14–15	Ps. *3*; 7 *alt.* Ps. *88*; (95) Gen. ch. 40 Gal. 3. 1–14	Ps. 31 *alt.* Ps. 102 Jer. 3. 6–22 John 4. 27–42

5 Saturday

P		Isa. 58. 9b–end Ps. 86. 1–7 Luke 5. 27–32	Ps. 71 *alt.* Ps. 96; *97*; 100 Gen. 41. 1–24 Gal. 3. 15–22	Ps. 73 Jer. 4. 1–18 John 4. 43–end ct

6 Sunday   THE FIRST SUNDAY OF LENT

P		Deut. 26. 1–11 Ps. 91. 1–2, 9–end (*or* 91. 1–11) Rom. 10. 8b–13 Luke 4. 1–13	Ps. 50. 1–15 Mic. 6. 1–8 Luke 5. 27–end	Ps. 119. 73–88 Jonah ch. 3 Luke 18. 9–14

	Calendar and Holy Communion	Morning Prayer	Evening Prayer
	QUINQUAGESIMA		
G	Gen. 9. 8–17 Ps. 77. 11–end 1 Cor. ch. 13 Luke 18. 31–43	Ps. 2 Exod. 33. 17–end Luke 9. 28–43	Ps. 89. 1–18 (or 89. 5–12) Exod. 3. 1–6 John 12. 27–36a
G		Gen. 37. 1–11 Gal. ch. 1	Jer. ch. 1 John 3. 1–21

NOTES

David, Bishop of Menevia, Patron of Wales, c. 601

Gw	Com. Bishop	Gen. 37. 12–end Gal. 2. 1–10	Jer. 2. 1–13 John 3. 22–end

ASH WEDNESDAY

P	Ash Wednesday Collect until 16 April Commination Joel 2. 12–17 Ps. 57 Jas. 4. 1–10 Matt. 6. 16–21	Ps. 38 Dan. 9. 3–6, 17–19 1 Tim. 6. 6–19	Ps. 51 or Ps. 102 (or 102. 1–18) Isa. 1. 10–18 Luke 15. 11–end
P	Exod. 24. 12–end Matt. 8. 5–13	Gen. ch. 39 Gal. 2. 11–end	Jer. 2. 14–32 John 4. 1–26
P	1 Kings 19. 3b–8 Matt. 5.43 – 6.6	Gen. ch. 40 Gal. 3. 1–14	Jer. 3. 6–22 John 4. 27–42
P	Isa. 38. 1–6a Mark 6. 45–end	Gen. 41. 1–24 Gal. 3. 15–22	Jer. 4. 1–18 John 4. 43–end
			ct

	THE FIRST SUNDAY IN LENT		
P	Collect (1) Lent 1 (2) Ash Wednesday Ember until 12 March Gen. 3. 1–6 Ps. 91. 1–12 2 Cor. 6. 1–10 Matt. 4. 1–11	Ps. 50. 1–15 Mic. 6. 1–8 Luke 5. 27–end	Ps. 119. 73–88 Jonah ch. 3 Luke 18. 9–14

	Sunday Principal Service / Weekday Eucharist	Third Service / Morning Prayer	Second Service / Evening Prayer

7 Monday — Perpetua, Felicity and their Companions, Martyrs at Carthage, 203

Pr

	Com. Martyr *or* Lev. 19. 1–2, 11–18	Ps. 10; **11**	Ps. 12; **13**; 14
	esp. Rev. 12. 10–12a Ps. 19. 7–end	*alt.* Ps. **98**; 99; 101	*alt.* Ps. **105**† (*or* 103)
	also Wisd. 3. 1–7 Matt. 25. 31–end	Gen. 41. 25–45	Jer. 4. 19–end
		Gal. 3.23 – 4.7	John 5. 1–18

8 Tuesday — Edward King, Bishop of Lincoln, 1910
Felix, Bishop, Apostle to the East Angles, 647; Geoffrey Studdert Kennedy, Priest, Poet, 1929

Pw

	Com. Bishop *or* Isa. 55. 10–11	Ps. 44	Ps. 46; **49**
	also Heb. 13. 1–8 Ps. 34. 4–6, 21–22	*alt.* Ps. **106**† (*or* 103)	*alt.* Ps. 107†
	Matt. 6. 7–15	Gen. 41.46 – 42.5	Jer. 5. 1–19
		Gal. 4. 8–20	John 5. 19–29

9 Wednesday — Ember Day*

P

	Jonah ch. 3	Ps. **6**; 17	Ps. 9; **28**
	Ps. 51. 1–5, 17–18	*alt.* Ps. 110; **111**; 112	*alt.* Ps. 119. 129–152
	Luke 11. 29–32	Gen. 42. 6–17	Jer. 5. 20–end
		Gal. 4.21 – 5.1	John 5. 30–end

10 Thursday

P

	Esther 14. 1–5, 12–14	Ps. **42**; 43	Ps. 137; 138; **142**
	or Isa. 55. 6–9	*alt.* Ps. 113; **115**	*alt.* Ps. 114; **116**; 117
	Ps. 138	Gen. 42. 18–28	Jer. 6. 9–21
	Matt. 7. 7–12	Gal. 5. 2–15	John 6. 1–15

11 Friday — Ember Day*

P

	Ezek. 18. 21–28	Ps. 22	Ps. 54; **55**
	Ps. 130	*alt.* Ps. 139	*alt.* Ps. **130**; 131; 137
	Matt. 5. 20–26	Gen. 42. 29–end	Jer. 6. 22–end
		Gal. 5. 16–end	John 6. 16–27

12 Saturday — Ember Day*

P

	Deut. 26. 16–end	Ps. 59; **63**	Ps. **4**; 16
	Ps. 119. 1–8	*alt.* Ps. 120; **121**; 122	*alt.* Ps. 118
	Matt. 5. 43–end	Gen. 43. 1–15	Jer. 7. 1–20
		Gal. ch. 6	John 6. 27–40

ct

13 Sunday — THE SECOND SUNDAY OF LENT

P

	Gen. 15. 1–12, 17–18	Ps. 119. 161–end	Ps. 135 (*or* 135. 1–14)
	Ps. 27	Gen. 17. 1–7, 15–16	Jer. 22. 1–9, 13–17
	Phil. 3.17 – 4.1	Rom. 11. 13–24	Luke 14. 27–33
	Luke 13. 31–end		

14 Monday

P

	Dan. 9. 4–10	Ps. 26; **32**	Ps. 70; **74**
	Ps. 79. 8–9, 12, 14	*alt.* Ps. 123; 124; 125; **126**	alt. *Ps.* **127**; 128; 129
	Luke 6. 36–38	Gen. 43. 16–end	Jer. 7. 21–end
		Heb. ch. 1	John 6. 41–51

15 Tuesday

P

	Isa. 1. 10, 16–20	Ps. 50	Ps. **52**; 53; 54
	Ps. 50. 8, 16–end	*alt.* Ps. **132**; 133	*alt.* Ps. (134); **135**
	Matt. 23. 1–12	Gen. 44. 1–17	Jer. 8. 1–15
		Heb. 2. 1–9	John 6. 52–59

*For Ember Day provision, see p. 11.

	Calendar and Holy Communion	Morning Prayer	Evening Prayer	NOTES
	Perpetua, Martyr at Carthage, 203			
Pr	Com. Martyr or Ezek. 34. 11–16a Matt. 25. 31–end	Gen. 41. 25–45 Gal. 3.23 – 4.7	Jer. 4. 19–end John 5. 1–18	
P	Isa. 55. 6–11 Matt. 21. 10–16	Gen. 41.46 – 42.5 Gal. 4. 8–20	Jer. 5. 1–19 John 5. 19–29	
	Ember Day			
P	Ember CEG or Isa. 58. 1–9a Matt. 12. 38–end	Gen. 42. 6–17 Gal. 4.21 – 5.1	Jer. 5. 20–end John 5. 30–end	
P	Isa. 58. 9b–end John 8. 31–45	Gen. 42. 18–28 Gal. 5. 2–15	Jer. 6. 9–21 John 6. 1–15	
	Ember Day			
P	Ember CEG or Ezek. 18. 20–25 John 5. 2–15	Gen. 42. 29–end Gal. 5. 16–end	Jer. 6. 22–end John 6. 16–27	
	Gregory the Great, Bishop of Rome, 604 Ember Day			
Pw	Ember CEG or Com. Doctor or Ezek. 18. 26–end Matt. 17. 1–9 or Luke 4. 16–21 or John 10. 1–16	Gen. 43. 1–15 Gal. ch. 6	Jer. 7. 1–20 John 6. 27–40 ct	
	THE SECOND SUNDAY IN LENT			
P	Jer. 17. 5–10 Ps. 25. 13–end 1 Thess. 4. 1–8 Matt. 15. 21–28	Ps. 119. 161–end Gen. 17. 1–7, 15–16 Rom. 11. 13–24	Ps. 135 (or 135. 1–14) Jer. 22. 1–9, 13–17 Luke 14. 27–33	
P	Heb. 2. 1–10 John 8. 21–30	Gen. 43. 16–end Heb. ch. 1	Jer. 7. 21–end John 6. 41–51	
P	Heb. 2. 11–end Matt. 23. 1–12	Gen. 44. 1–17 Heb. 2. 1–9	Jer. 8. 1–15 John 6. 52–59	

		Sunday Principal Service Weekday Eucharist	Third Service Morning Prayer	Second Service Evening Prayer
16 Wednesday				
P		Jer. 18. 18–20 Ps. 31. 4–5, 14–18 Matt. 20. 17–28	Ps. 35 *alt.* Ps. 119. 153–end Gen. 44. 18–end Heb. 2. 10–end	Ps. *3*; 51 *alt.* Ps. 136 Jer. 8.18 – 9.11 John 6. 60–end
17 Thursday	Patrick, Bishop, Missionary, Patron of Ireland, c. 460			
Pw	Com. Missionary *or* *also* Ps. 91. 1–4, 13–end Luke 10. 1–12, 17–20	Jer. 17. 5–10 Ps. 1 Luke 16. 19–end	Ps. 34 *alt.* Ps. *143*; 146 Gen. 45. 1–15 Heb. 3. 1–6	Ps. 71 *alt.* Ps. *138*; 140; 141 Jer. 9. 12–24 John 7. 1–13
18 Friday	Cyril, Bishop of Jerusalem, Teacher, 386			
P		Gen. 37. 3–4, 12–13, 17–28 Ps. 105. 16–22 Matt. 21. 33–43, 45–46	Ps. 40; *41* *alt.* Ps. 142; *144* Gen. 45. 16–end Heb. 3. 7–end	Ps. *6*; 38 *alt.* Ps. 145 Jer. 10. 1–16 John 7. 14–24 *or First EP of Joseph* Ps. 132 Hos. 11. 1–9 Luke 2. 41–end **W ct**
19 Saturday	**JOSEPH OF NAZARETH**			
W		2 Sam. 7. 4–16 Ps. 89. 26–36 Rom. 4. 13–18 Matt. 1. 18–end	*MP*: Ps. 25; 147. 1–12 Isa. 11. 1–10 Matt. 13. 54–end	*EP*: Ps. 1; 112 Gen. 50. 22–end Matt. 2. 13–end
20 Sunday	**THE THIRD SUNDAY OF LENT**			
P		Isa. 55. 1–9 Ps. 63. 1–9 1 Cor. 10. 1–13 Luke 13. 1–9	Ps. 26; 28 Deut. 6. 4–9 John 17. 1a, 11b–19	Ps. 12; 13 Gen. 28. 10–19a John 1. 35–end
21 Monday*	**Thomas Cranmer, Archbishop of Canterbury, Reformation Martyr, 1556**			
Pr	Com. Martyr *or*	2 Kings 5. 1–15 Ps. 42. 1–2; 43. 1–4 Luke 4. 24–30	Ps. *5*; 7 *alt.* Ps. *1*; 2; 3 Gen. 47. 1–27 Heb. 4.14 – 5.10	Ps. 11; *17* *alt.* Ps. *4*; 7 Jer. 11. 1–17 John 7. 37–52
22 Tuesday				
P		Song of the Three 2, 11–20 *or* Dan. 2. 20–23 Ps. 25. 3–10 Matt. 18. 21–end	Ps. 6; *9* *alt.* Ps. *5*; 6; (8) Gen. 47.28 – 48.end Heb. 5.11 – 6.12	Ps. 61; 62; *64* *alt.* Ps. *9*; 10† Jer. 11.18 – 12.6 John 7.53 – 8.11
23 Wednesday				
P		Deut. 4. 1, 5–9 Ps. 147. 13–end Matt. 5. 17–19	Ps. 38 *alt.* Ps. 119. 1–32 Gen. 49. 1–32 Heb. 6. 13–end	Ps. 36; *39* *alt.* Ps. *11*; 12; 13 Jer. 13. 1–11 John 8. 12–30

*The following readings may replace those provided for Holy Communion on any day (except The Annunciation) during the Third Week of Lent: Exod. 17. 1–7; Ps. 95. 1–2, 6–end; John 4. 5–42.

	Calendar and Holy Communion	Morning Prayer	Evening Prayer	NOTES
P	Heb. 3. 1–6 Matt. 20. 17–28	Gen. 44. 18–end Heb. 2. 10–end	Jer. 8.18 – 9.11 John 6. 60–end	
P	Heb. 3. 7–end John 5. 30–end	Gen. 45. 1–15 Heb. 3. 1–6	Jer. 9. 12–24 John 7. 1–13	

Edward, King of the West Saxons, 978

Pr	Com. Martyr or Heb. ch. 4 Matt. 21. 33–end	Gen. 45. 16–end Heb. 3. 7–end	Jer. 10. 1–16 John 7. 14–24	

To celebrate Joseph, see *Common Worship* provision.

P	Heb. ch. 5 Luke 15. 11–end	Gen. 46. 1–7, 28–end Heb. 4. 1–13	Jer. 10. 17–24 John 7. 25–36	

ct

THE THIRD SUNDAY IN LENT

P	Num. 22. 21–31 Ps. 9. 13–end Eph. 5. 1–14 Luke 11. 14–28	Ps. 26; 28 Deut. 6. 4–9 John 17. 1a, 11b–19	Ps. 12; 13 Gen. 28. 10–19a John 1. 35–end	

Benedict, Abbot of Monte Casino, c. 550

Pw	Com. Abbot or Heb. 6. 1–10 Luke 4. 23–30	Gen. 47. 1–27 Heb. 4.14 – 5.10	Jer. 11. 1–17 John 7. 37–52	
P	Heb. 6. 11–end Matt. 18. 15–22	Gen. 47.28 – 48.end Heb. 5.11 – 6.12	Jer. 11.18 – 12.6 John 7.53 – 8.11	
P	Heb. 7. 1–10 Matt. 15. 1–20	Gen. 49. 1–32 Heb. 6. 13–end	Jer. 13. 1–11 John 8. 12–30	

	Sunday Principal Service Weekday Eucharist	Third Service Morning Prayer	Second Service Evening Prayer
24 Thursday	*Walter Hilton of Thurgarton, Augustinian Canon, Mystic, 1396; Paul Couturier, Priest, Ecumenist, 1953; Oscar Romero, Archbishop of San Salvador, Martyr, 1980*		
P	Jer. 7. 23–28 Ps. 95. 1–2, 6–end Luke 11. 14–23	Ps. **56**; 57 *alt.* Ps. 14; **15**; 16 Gen. 49.33 – 50.end Heb. 7. 1–10	*First EP of The Annunciation* Ps. 85 Wisd. 9. 1–12 *or* Gen. 3. 8–15 Gal. 4. 1–5 𝖂 ct
25 Friday	**THE ANNUNCIATION OF OUR LORD TO THE BLESSED VIRGIN MARY**		
𝖂	Isa. 7. 10–14 Ps. 40. 5–11 Heb. 10. 4–10 Luke 1. 26–38	*MP*: Ps. 111; 113 1 Sam. 2. 1–10 Rom. 5. 12–end	*EP*: Ps. 131; 146 Isa. 52. 1–12 Heb. 2. 5–end
26 Saturday	*Harriet Monsell, Founder of the Community of St John the Baptist, Clewer, 1883*		
P	Hos. 5.15 – 6.6 Ps. 51. 1–2, 17–end Luke 18. 9–14	Ps. 31 *alt.* Ps. 20; 21; **23** Exod. 1.22 – 2.10 Heb. ch. 8	Ps. **116**; 130 *alt.* Ps. **24**; 25 Jer. 16.10 – 17.4 John 9. 1–17 ct
27 Sunday	**THE FOURTH SUNDAY OF LENT** (Mothering Sunday)		
P	Josh. 5. 9–12 Ps. 32 2 Cor. 5. 16–end Luke 15. 1–3, 11b–end	Ps. 84; 85 Gen. 37. 3–4, 12–end 1 Pet. 2. 16–end	Ps. 30 Prayer of Manasseh *or* Isa. 40.27 – 41.13 2 Tim. 4. 1–18 *Gospel*: John 11. 17–44 *If the Principal Service readings for The Fourth Sunday of Lent are displaced by Mothering Sunday provisions, they may be used at the Second Service.*
	or, for Mothering Sunday: Exod. 2. 1–10 *or* 1 Sam. 1. 20–end Ps. 34. 11–20 *or* Ps. 127. 1–4 2 Cor. 1. 3–7 *or* Col. 3. 12–17 Luke 2. 33–35 *or* John 19. 25b–27		
28 Monday*			
P	Isa. 65. 17–21 Ps. 30. 1–5, 8, 11–end John 4. 43–end	Ps. 70; **77** *alt.* Ps. 27; **30** Exod. 2. 11–22 Heb. 9. 1–14	Ps. **25**; 28 *alt.* Ps. 26; **28**; 29 Jer. 17. 5–18 John 9. 18–end
29 Tuesday			
P	Ezek. 47. 1–9, 12 Ps. 46. 1–8 John 5. 1–3, 5–16	Ps. 54; **79** *alt.* Ps. 32; **36** Exod. 2.23 – 3.20 Heb. 9. 15–end	Ps. **80**; 82 *alt.* Ps. 33 Jer. 18. 1–12 John 10. 1–10

*The following readings may replace those provided for Holy Communion on any day during the Fourth Week of Lent: Mic. 7. 7–9; Ps. 27. 1, 9–10, 16–17; John ch. 9.

	Calendar and Holy Communion	Morning Prayer	Evening Prayer	NOTES
P	Heb. 7. 11–25 John 6. 26–35	Gen. 49.33 – 50.end Heb. 7. 1–10	*First EP of The* *Annunciation* Ps. 85 Wisd. 9. 1–12 *or* Gen. 3. 8–15 Gal. 4. 1–5 𝔚 ct	

THE ANNUNCIATION OF THE BLESSED VIRGIN MARY

	Calendar and Holy Communion	Morning Prayer	Evening Prayer	NOTES
𝔚	Isa. 7. 10–14 [15] Ps. 113 Rom. 5. 12–19 Luke 1. 26–38	Ps. 111 1 Sam. 2. 1–10 Heb. 10. 4–10	Ps. 131; 146 Isa. 52. 1–12 Heb. 2. 5–end	
P	Heb. 8. 1–6 John 8. 1–11	Exod. 1.22 – 2.10 Heb. ch. 8	Jer. 16.10 – 17.4 John 9. 1–17	
			ct	

THE FOURTH SUNDAY IN LENT
To celebrate Mothering Sunday, *see Common Worship* provision.

	Calendar and Holy Communion	Morning Prayer	Evening Prayer	NOTES
P	Exod. 16. 2–7a Ps. 122 Gal. 4. 21–end *or* Heb. 12. 22–24 John 6. 1–14	Ps. 84; 85 Gen. 37. 3–4, 12–end 1 Pet. 2. 16–end	Ps. 30 Prayer of Manasseh *or* Isa. 40.27 – 41.13 2 Tim. 4. 1–18	
P	Heb. 11. 1–6 John 2. 13–end	Exod. 2. 11–22 Heb. 9. 1–14	Jer. 17. 5–18 John 9. 18–end	
P	Heb. 11. 13–16a John 7. 14–24	Exod. 2.23 – 3.20 Heb. 9. 15–end	Jer. 18. 1–12 John 10. 1–10	

	Sunday Principal Service / Weekday Eucharist	Third Service / Morning Prayer	Second Service / Evening Prayer
30 Wednesday			
P	Isa. 49. 8–15 Ps. 145. 8–18 John 5. 17–30	Ps. **63**; 90 *alt.* Ps. 34 Exod. 4. 1–23 Heb. 10. 1–18	Ps. 52; **91** *alt.* Ps. 119. 33–56 Jer. 18. 13–end John 10. 11–21
31 Thursday *John Donne, Priest, Poet, 1631*			
P	Exod. 32. 7–14 Ps. 106. 19–23 John 5. 31–end	Ps. 53; **86** *alt.* Ps. 37† Exod. 4.27 – 6.1 Heb. 10. 19–25	Ps. 94 *alt.* Ps. 39; **40** Jer. 19. 1–13 John 10. 22–end

April 2022

	Sunday Principal Service / Weekday Eucharist	Third Service / Morning Prayer	Second Service / Evening Prayer
1 Friday *Frederick Denison Maurice, Priest, Teacher, 1872*			
P	Wisd. 2. 1, 12–22 *or* Jer. 26. 8–11 Ps. 34. 15–end John 7. 1–2, 10, 25–30	Ps. 102 *alt.* Ps. 31 Exod. 6. 2–13 Heb. 10. 26–end	Ps. 13; **16** *alt.* Ps. 35 Jer. 19.14 – 20.6 John 11. 1–16
2 Saturday			
P	Jer. 11. 18–20 Ps. 7. 1–2, 8–10 John 7. 40–52	Ps. 32 *alt.* Ps. 41; **42**; 43 Exod. 7. 8–end Heb. 11. 1–16	Ps. **140**; 141; 142 *alt.* Ps. 45; **46** Jer. 20. 7–end John 11. 17–27 **ct**
3 Sunday **THE FIFTH SUNDAY OF LENT (Passiontide begins)**			
P	Isa. 43. 16–21 Ps. 126 Phil. 3. 4b–14 John 12. 1–8	Ps. 111; 112 Isa. ch. 35 Rom. 7.21 – 8.4	Ps. 35 (*or* 35. 1–9) 2 Chron. 35. 1–6, 10–16 Luke 22. 1–13
4 Monday*			
P	Susanna 1–9, 15–17, 19–30, 33–62 (*or* 41b–62) *or* Josh. 2. 1–14 Ps. 23 John 8. 31–42	Ps. **73**; 121 *alt.* Ps. 44 Exod. 8. 1–19 Heb. 11. 17–31	Ps. **26**; 27 *alt.* Ps. **47**; 49 Jer. 21. 1–10 John 11. 28–44
5 Tuesday			
P	Num. 21. 4–9 Ps. 102. 1–3, 16–23 John 8. 21–30	Ps. **35**; 123 *alt.* Ps. **48**; 52 Exod. 8. 20–end Heb. 11.32 – 12.2	Ps. **61**; 64 *alt.* Ps. 50 Jer. 22. 1–5, 13–19 John 11. 45–end
6 Wednesday			
P	Dan. 3. 14–20, 24–25, 28 *Canticle*: Bless the Lord John 8. 31–42	Ps. **55**; 124 *alt.* Ps. 119. 57–80 Exod. 9. 1–12 Heb. 12. 3–13	Ps. 56; **62** *alt.* Ps. **59**; 60 (67) Jer. 22.20 – 23.8 John 12. 1–11

*The following readings may replace those provided for Holy Communion on any day during the Fifth Week of Lent: 2 Kings 4. 18–21, 32–37; Ps. 17. 1–8, 16; John 11. 1–45.

	Calendar and Holy Communion	Morning Prayer	Evening Prayer	NOTES
P	Heb. 12. 1–11 John 9. 1–17	Exod. 4. 1–23 Heb. 10. 1–18	Jer. 18. 13–end John 10. 11–21	
P	Heb. 12. 12–17 John 5. 17–27	Exod. 4.27 – 6.1 Heb. 10. 19–25	Jer. 19. 1–13 John 10. 22–end	
P	Heb. 12. 22–end John 11. 33–46	Exod. 6. 2–13 Heb. 10. 26–end	Jer. 19.14 – 20.6 John 11. 1–16	
P	Heb. 13. 17–21 John 8. 12–20	Exod. 7. 8–end Heb. 11. 1–16	Jer. 20. 7–end John 11. 17–27	
			ct	

THE FIFTH SUNDAY IN LENT

P	Exod. 24. 4–8 Ps. 143 Heb. 9. 11–15 John 8. 46–end	Ps. 111; 112 Isa. ch. 35 Rom. 7.21 – 8.4	Ps. 35 (or 35. 1–9) 2 Chron. 35. 1–6, 10–16 Luke 22. 1–13	

Ambrose, Bishop of Milan, 397

Pw	Com. Doctor or Col. 1. 13–23a John 7. 1–13	Exod. 8. 1–19 Heb. 11. 17–31	Jer. 21. 1–10 John 11. 28–44	
P	Col. 2. 8–12 John 7. 32–39	Exod. 8. 20–end Heb. 11.32 – 12.2	Jer. 22. 1–5, 13–19 John 11. 45–end	
P	Col. 2. 13–19 John 7. 40–end	Exod. 9. 1–12 Heb. 12. 3–13	Jer. 22.20 – 23.8 John 12. 1–11	

		Sunday Principal Service Weekday Eucharist	Third Service Morning Prayer	Second Service Evening Prayer
7 Thursday				
P		Gen. 17. 3–9 Ps. 105. 4–9 John 8. 51–end	Ps. *40*; 125 *alt.* Ps. 56; *57*; (63†) Exod. 9. 13–end Heb. 12. 14–end	Ps. 42; *43* *alt.* Ps. 61; *62*; 64 Jer. 23. 9–32 John 12. 12–19
8 Friday				
P		Jer. 20. 10–13 Ps. 18. 1–6 John 10. 31–end	Ps. *22*; 126 *alt.* Ps. *51*; 54 Exod. ch. 10 Heb. 13. 1–16	Ps. 31 *alt.* Ps. 38 Jer. ch. 24 John 12. 20–36a
9 Saturday	*Dietrich Bonhoeffer, Lutheran Pastor, Martyr, 1945*			
P		Ezek. 37. 21–end *Canticle:* Jer. 31. 10–13 *or* Ps. 121 John 11. 45–end	Ps. *23*; 127 *alt.* Ps. 68 Exod. ch. 11 Heb. 13. 17–end	Ps. 128; 129; *130* *alt.* Ps. 65; *66* Jer. 25. 1–14 John 12. 36b–end ct
10 Sunday	**PALM SUNDAY**			
R		*Liturgy of the Palms* Luke 19. 28–40 Ps. 118. 1–2, 19–end (*or* 118. 19–24)	*Liturgy of the Passion* Isa. 50. 4–9a Ps. 31. 9–16 (*or* 31. 9–18) Phil. 2. 5–11 Luke 22.14 – 23.end *or* Luke 23. 1–49	Ps. 61; 62 Zech. 9. 9–12 1 Cor. 2. 1–12	Ps. 69. 1–20 Isa. 5. 1–7 Luke 20. 9–19
11 Monday	**MONDAY OF HOLY WEEK**			
R		Isa. 42. 1–9 Ps. 36. 5–11 Heb. 9. 11–15 John 12. 1–11	*MP*: Ps. 41 Lam. 1. 1–12a Luke 22. 1–23	*EP*: Ps. 25 Lam. 2. 8–19 Col. 1. 18–23
12 Tuesday	**TUESDAY OF HOLY WEEK**			
R		Isa. 49. 1–7 Ps. 71. 1–14 (*or* 71. 1–8) 1 Cor. 1. 18–31 John 12. 20–36	*MP*: Ps. 27 Lam. 3. 1–18 Luke 22. [24–38] 39–53	*EP*: Ps. 55. 13–24 Lam. 3. 40–51 Gal. 6. 11–end
13 Wednesday	**WEDNESDAY OF HOLY WEEK**			
R		Isa. 50. 4–9a Ps. 70 Heb. 12. 1–3 John 13. 21–32	*MP*: Ps. 102 (*or* 102. 1–18) Wisd. 1.16 – 2.1, 12–22 *or* Jer. 11. 18–20 Luke 22. 54–end	*EP*: Ps. 88 Isa. 63. 1–9 Rev. 14.18 – 15.4
14 Thursday	**MAUNDY THURSDAY**			
W (HC) R		Exod. 12. 1–4 [5–10], 11–14 Ps. 116. 1, 10–end (*or* 116. 9–end) 1 Cor. 11. 23–26 John 13. 1–17, 31b–35	*MP*: Ps. 42; 43 Lev. 16. 2–24 Luke 23. 1–25	*EP*: Ps. 39 Exod. ch. 11 Eph. 2. 11–18

	Calendar and Holy Communion	Morning Prayer	Evening Prayer	NOTES
P	Col. 3. 8–11 John 10. 22–38	Exod. 9. 13–end Heb. 12. 14–end	Jer. 23. 9–32 John 12. 12–19	
P	Col. 3. 12–17 John 11. 47–54	Exod. ch. 10 Heb. 13. 1–16	Jer. ch. 24 John 12. 20–36a	
P	Col. 4. 2–6 John 6. 53–end	Exod. ch. 11 Heb. 13. 17–end	Jer. 25. 1–14 John 12. 36b–end	
			ct	

THE SUNDAY NEXT BEFORE EASTER (PALM SUNDAY)

R	Zech. 9. 9–12 Ps. 73. 22–end Phil. 2. 5–11 Passion acc. to Matthew Matt. 27. 1–54 *or* Matt. 26.1 – 27.61 *or* Matt. 21. 1–13	Ps. 61; 62 Zech. 9. 9–12 1 Cor. 2. 1–12	Ps. 69. 1–20 Isa. 5. 1–7 Luke 20. 9–19	

MONDAY IN HOLY WEEK

R	Isa. 63. 1–19 Ps. 55. 1–8 Gal. 6. 1–11 Mark ch. 14	Ps. 41 Lam. 1. 1–12a John 12. 1–11	Ps. 25 Lam. 2. 8–19 Col. 1. 18–23	

TUESDAY IN HOLY WEEK

R	Isa. 50. 5–11 Ps. 13 Rom. 5. 6–19 Mark 15. 1–39	Ps. 27 Lam. 3. 1–18 John 12. 20–36	Ps. 55. 13–24 Lam. 3. 40–51 Gal. 6. 11–end	

WEDNESDAY IN HOLY WEEK

R	Isa. 49. 1–9a Ps. 54 Heb. 9. 16–end Luke ch. 22	Ps. 102 (*or* 102. 1–18) Wisd. 1.16 – 2.1, 12–22 *or* Jer. 11. 18–20 John 13. 21–32	Ps. 88 Isa. 63. 1–9 Rev. 14.18 – 15.4	

MAUNDY THURSDAY

W **(HC)** **R**	Exod. 12. 1–11 Ps. 43 1 Cor. 11. 17–end Luke 23. 1–49	Ps. 42; 43 Lev. 16. 2–24 John 13. 1–17, 31b–35	Ps. 39 Exod. ch. 11 Eph. 2. 11–18	

		Sunday Principal Service / Weekday Eucharist	Third Service / Morning Prayer	Second Service / Evening Prayer

15 Friday — GOOD FRIDAY

		Sunday Principal Service / Weekday Eucharist	Third Service / Morning Prayer	Second Service / Evening Prayer
R		Isa. 52.13 – 53.end Ps. 22 (or 22. 1–11 or 22. 1–21) Heb. 10. 16–25 or Heb. 4. 14–16; 5. 7–9 John 18.1 – 19.end	*MP*: Ps. 69 Gen. 22. 1–18 *A part of John 18 – 19 if not read at the Principal Service* or Heb. 10. 1–10	*EP*: Ps. 130; 143 Lam. 5. 15–end *A part of John 18 – 19 if not read at the Principal Service,* *esp.* John 19. 38–end or Col. 1. 18–23

16 Saturday — EASTER EVE

	These readings are for use at services other than the Easter Vigil.	Job 14. 1–14 or Lam. 3. 1–9, 19–24 Ps. 31. 1–4, 15–16 (or 31. 1–5) 1 Pet. 4. 1–8 Matt. 27. 57–end or John 19. 38–end	Ps. 142 Hos. 6. 1–6 John 2. 18–22	Ps. 116 Job 19. 21–27 1 John 5. 5–12

17 Sunday — EASTER DAY

w	*The following readings and psalms (or canticles) are provided for use at the Easter Vigil. A minimum of three Old Testament readings should be chosen. The reading from Exodus ch. 14 should always be used.*	Gen. 1.1 – 2.4a & Ps. 136. 1–9, 23–end Gen. 7. 1–5, 11–18; 8. 6–18; 9. 8–13 & Ps. 46 Gen. 22. 1–18 & Ps. 16 Exod. 14. 10–end; 15. 20–21 & Canticle: Exod. 15. 1b–13, 17–18 Isa. 55. 1–11 & Canticle: Isa. 12. 2–end Baruch 3.9–15, 32 – 4.4 & Ps. 19 or Prov. 8. 1–8, 19–21; 9. 4b–6 & Ps. 19 Ezek. 36. 24–28 & Ps. 42; 43 Ezek. 37. 1–14 & Ps. 143 Zeph. 3. 14–end & Ps. 98 Rom. 6. 3–11 & Ps. 114 Luke 24. 1–12		
w	*Easter Day Services* The reading from Acts must be used as either the first or second reading at the Principal Service.	Acts 10. 34–43 or Isa. 65. 17–end Ps. 118. 1–2, 14–24 (or 118. 14–24) 1 Cor. 15. 19–26 or Acts 10. 34–43 John 20. 1–18 or Luke 24. 1–12	*MP*: Ps. 114; 117 Ezek. 47. 1–12 John 2. 13–22	*EP*: Ps. 105 or Ps. 66. 1–11 Isa. 43. 1–21 1 Cor. 15. 1–11 or John 20. 19–23

18 Monday — MONDAY OF EASTER WEEK

W		Acts 2. 14, 22–32 Ps. 16. 1–2, 6–end Matt. 28. 8–15	Ps. *111*; 117; 146 Exod. 12. 1–14 1 Cor. 15. 1–11	Ps. 135 Song of Sol. 1.9 – 2.7 Mark 16. 1–8

19 Tuesday — TUESDAY OF EASTER WEEK

W		Acts 2. 36–41 Ps. 33. 4–5, 18–end John 20. 11–18	Ps. *112*; 147. 1–12 Exod. 12. 14–36 1 Cor. 15. 12–19	Ps. 136 Song of Sol. 2. 8–end Luke 24. 1–12

20 Wednesday — WEDNESDAY OF EASTER WEEK

W		Acts 3. 1–10 Ps. 105. 1–9 Luke 24. 13–35	Ps. *113*; 147. 13–end Exod. 12. 37–end 1 Cor. 15. 20–28	Ps. 105 Song of Sol. ch. 3 Matt. 28. 16–end

	Calendar and Holy Communion	Morning Prayer	Evening Prayer	NOTES
	GOOD FRIDAY			
R	Alt. Collect Passion acc. to John Alt. Gospel, if Passion is read Num. 21. 4–9 Ps. 140. 1–9 Heb. 10. 1–25 John 19. 1–37 *or* John 19. 38–end	Ps. 69 Gen. 22. 1–18 John ch. 18	Ps. 130; 143 Lam. 5. 15–end John 19. 38–end	
	EASTER EVE			
	Job 14. 1–14 1 Pet. 3. 17–22 Matt. 27. 57–end	Ps. 142 Hos. 6. 1–6 John 2. 18–22	Ps. 116 Job 19. 21–27 1 John 5. 5–12	
	EASTER DAY			
𝔴	Exod. 12. 21–28 Ps. 111 Col. 3. 1–7 John 20. 1–10	Ps. 114; 117 Ezek. 47. 1–12 John 2. 13–22	Ps. 105 *or* Ps. 66. 1–11 Isa. 43. 1–21 1 Cor. 15. 1–11 *or* John 20. 19–23	
	MONDAY IN EASTER WEEK			
W	Hos. 6. 1–6 Easter Anthems Acts 10. 34–43 Luke 24. 13–35	Exod. 12. 1–14 1 Cor. 15. 1–11	Song of Sol. 1.9 – 2.7 Mark 16. 1–8	
	TUESDAY IN EASTER WEEK			
W	1 Kings 17. 17–end Ps. 16. 9–end Acts 13. 26–41 Luke 24. 36b–48	Exod. 12. 14–36 1 Cor. 15. 12–19	Song of Sol. 2. 8–end Luke 24. 1–12	
W	Isa. 42. 10–16 Ps. 111 Acts 3. 12–18 John 20. 11–18	Exod. 12. 37–end 1 Cor. 15. 20–28	Song of Sol. ch. 3 Matt. 28. 16–end	

		Sunday Principal Service / Weekday Eucharist	Third Service / Morning Prayer	Second Service / Evening Prayer

21 Thursday — **THURSDAY OF EASTER WEEK**

W		Acts 3. 11–end	Ps. *114*; 148	Ps. 106
		Ps. 8	Exod. 13. 1–16	Song of Sol. 5.2 – 6.3
		Luke 24. 35–48	1 Cor. 15. 29–34	Luke 7. 11–17

22 Friday — **FRIDAY OF EASTER WEEK**

W		Acts 4. 1–12	Ps. *115*; 149	Ps. 107
		Ps. 118. 1–4, 22–26	Exod. 13.17 – 14.14	Song of Sol. 7.10 – 8.4
		John 21. 1–14	1 Cor. 15. 35–50	Luke 8. 41–end

23 Saturday — **SATURDAY OF EASTER WEEK**
(George transferred to 26 April)

W		Acts 4. 13–21	Ps. *116*; 150	Ps. 145
		Ps. 118. 1–4, 14–21	Exod. 14. 15–end	Song of Sol. 8. 5–7
		Mark 16. 9–15	1 Cor. 15. 51–end	John 11. 17–44
				ct

24 Sunday — **THE SECOND SUNDAY OF EASTER**

W	*The reading from Acts must be used as either the first or second reading at the Principal Service.*	Acts 5. 27–32	Ps. 136. 1–16	Ps. 16
		[or Exod. 14. 10–end; 15. 20–21]	Exod. 12. 1–13	Isa. 52.13 – 53.12
		Ps. 118. 14–end	1 Pet. 1. 3–12	or 53. 1–6, 9–12
		or Ps. 150		Luke 24. 13–35
		Rev. 1. 4–8		*or First EP of Mark*
		John 20. 19–end		Ps. 19
				Isa. 52. 7–10
				Mark 1. 1–15
				R ct

25 Monday — **MARK THE EVANGELIST**

R		Prov. 15. 28–end	*MP*: Ps. 37. 23–end; 148	*EP*: Ps. 45
		or Acts 15. 35–end	Isa. 62. 6–10	Ezek. 1. 4–14
		Ps. 119. 9–16	or Ecclus. 51. 13–end	2 Tim. 4. 1–11
		Eph. 4. 7–16	Acts 12.25 – 13.13	*or first EP of George*
		Mark 13. 5–13		Ps. 111; 116
				Jer. 15. 15–end
				Heb. 11.32 – 12.2
				ct

26 Tuesday — **GEORGE, MARTYR, PATRON OF ENGLAND, c. 304**
(transferred from 23 April)

R		1 Macc. 2. 59–64	*MP*: Ps. 5; 146	*EP*: Ps. 3; 11
		or Rev. 12. 7–12	Josh. 1. 1–9	Isa. 43. 1–7
		Ps. 126	Eph. 6. 10–20	John 15. 1–8
		2 Tim. 2. 3–13		
		John 15. 18–21		

27 Wednesday — *Christina Rossetti, Poet, 1894*

W		Acts 5. 17–26	Ps. 16; *30*	Ps. 33
		Ps. 34. 1–8	*alt.* Ps. 119. 1–32	*alt.* Ps. *11*; 12; 13
		John 3. 16–21	Exod. 16. 11–end	Deut. 3. 18–end
			Col. 2. 1–15	John 20. 19–end

28 Thursday — *Peter Chanel, Missionary in the South Pacific, Martyr, 1841*

W		Acts 5. 27–33	Ps. *28*; 29	Ps. 34
		Ps. 34. 1, 15–end	*alt.* Ps. 14; *15*; 16	*alt.* Ps. 18†
		John 3. 31–end	Exod. ch. 17	Deut. 4. 1–14
			Col. 2.16 – 3.11	John 21. 1–14

	Calendar and Holy Communion	Morning Prayer	Evening Prayer	NOTES
W	Isa. 43. 16–21 Ps. 113 Acts 8. 26–end John 21. 1–14	Exod. 13. 1–16 1 Cor. 15. 29–34	Song of Sol. 5.2 – 6.3 Luke 7. 11–17	
W	Ezek. 37. 1–14 Ps. 116. 1–9 1 Pet. 3. 18–end Matt. 28. 16–end	Exod. 13.17 – 14.14 1 Cor. 15. 35–50	Song of Sol. 7.10 – 8.4 Luke 8. 41–end	
W	Zech. 8. 1–8 Ps. 118. 14–21 1 Pet. 2. 1–10 John 20. 24–end	Exod. 14. 15–end 1 Cor. 15. 51–end	Song of Sol. 8. 5–7 John 11. 17–44 **ct**	

THE FIRST SUNDAY AFTER EASTER

W	Ezek. 37. 1–10 Ps. 81. 1–4 1 John 5. 4–12 John 20. 19–23	Ps. 136. 1–16 Exod. 12. 1–13 1 Pet. 1. 3–12	Ps. 16 Isa. 52.13 – 53.12 or 53. 1–6, 9–12 Luke 24. 13–35 or First EP of Mark Ps. 19 Isa. 52. 7–10 Mark 1. 1–15 **R ct**	

MARK THE EVANGELIST

R	Prov. 15. 28–end Ps. 119. 9–16 Eph. 4. 7–16 John 15. 1–11	(Ps. 37. 23–end; 148) Isa. 62. 6–10 or Ecclus. 51. 13–end Acts 12.25 – 13.13	(Ps. 45) Ezek. 1. 4–14 2 Tim. 4. 1–11	

George, Martyr, Patron of England, c. 304
To celebrate George, see Common Worship provision.

Wr	Com. Martyr	Exod. 15.22 – 16.10 Col. 1. 15–end	Deut. 1. 19–40 John 20. 11–18	
W		Exod. 16. 11–end Col. 2. 1–15	Deut. 3. 18–end John 20. 19–end	
W		Exod. ch. 17 Col. 2.16 – 3.11	Deut. 4. 1–14 John 21. 1–14	

		Sunday Principal Service Weekday Eucharist	Third Service Morning Prayer	Second Service Evening Prayer
29 Friday	**Catherine of Siena, Teacher, 1380**			
W	Com. Teacher *or* *also* Prov. 8. 1, 6–11 John 17. 12–26	Acts 5. 34–42 Ps. 27. 1–5, 16–17 John 6. 1–15	Ps. 57; **61** *alt.* Ps. 17; **19** Exod. 18. 1–12 Col. 3.12 – 4.1	Ps. 118 *alt.* Ps. 22 Deut. 4. 15–31 John 21. 15–19
30 Saturday	*Pandita Mary Ramabai, Translator of the Scriptures, 1922*			
W		Acts 6. 1–7 Ps. 33. 1–5, 18–19 John 6. 16–21	Ps. 63; **84** *alt.* Ps. 20; 21; **23** Exod. 18. 13–end Col. 4. 2–end	Ps. 66 *alt.* Ps. **24**; 25 Deut. 4. 32–40 John 21. 20–end **ct**

May 2022

1 Sunday	**THE THIRD SUNDAY OF EASTER** (Philip and James transferred to 2 May)			
W	*The reading from* *Acts must be used* *as either the first or* *second reading at the* *Principal Service.*	Acts 9. 1–6 [7–20] [*or* Zeph. 3. 14–end] Ps. 30 Rev. 5. 11–end John 21. 1–19	Ps. 80. 1–8 Exod. 15. 1–2, 9–18 John 10. 1–19	Ps. 86 Isa. 38. 9–20 John 11. [17–26] 27–44 *or First EP of Philip and* *James* Ps. 25 Isa. 40. 27–end John 12. 20–26 **R ct**
2 Monday	**PHILIP AND JAMES, APOSTLES** (transferred from 1 May)			
R		Isa. 30. 15–21 Ps. 119. 1–8 Eph. 1. 3–10 John 14. 1–14	*MP*: Ps. 139; 146 Prov. 4. 10–18 Jas. 1. 1–12	*EP*: Ps. 149 Job 23. 1–12 John 1. 43–end
3 Tuesday				
W		Acts 7.51 – 8.1a Ps. 31. 1–5, 16 John 6. 30–35	Ps. **98**; 99; 100 *alt.* Ps. 32; **36** Exod. 20. 1–21 Luke 1. 26–38	Ps. 71 *alt.* Ps. 33 Deut. 5. 22–end Eph. 1. 15–end
4 Wednesday	**English Saints and Martyrs of the Reformation Era**			
W	Isa. 43. 1–7 *or* *or* Ecclus. 2. 10–17 Ps. 87 2 Cor. 4. 5–12 John 12. 20–26	Acts 8. 1b–8 Ps. 66. 1–6 John 6. 35–40	Ps. 105 *alt.* Ps. 34 Exod. ch. 24 Luke 1. 39–56	Ps. 67; **72** *alt.* Ps. 119. 33–56 Deut. ch. 6 Eph. 2. 1–10
5 Thursday				
W		Acts 8. 26–end Ps. 66. 7–8, 14–end John 6. 44–51	Ps. 136 *alt.* Ps. 37† Exod. 25. 1–22 Luke 1. 57–end	Ps. 73 *alt.* Ps. 39; **40** Deut. 7. 1–11 Eph. 2. 11–end
6 Friday				
W		Acts 9. 1–20 Ps. 117 John 6. 52–59	Ps. 107 *alt.* Ps. 31 Exod. 28. 1–4a, 29–38 Luke 2. 1–20	Ps. 77 *alt.* Ps. 35 Deut. 7. 12–end Eph. 3. 1–13

	Calendar and Holy Communion	Morning Prayer	Evening Prayer	NOTES
W		Exod. 18. 1–12 Col. 3.12 – 4.1	Deut. 4. 15–31 John 21. 15–19	
W		Exod. 18. 13–end Col. 4. 2–end	Deut. 4. 32–40 John 21. 20–end	
			ct	

	THE SECOND SUNDAY AFTER EASTER (Philip and James transferred to 2 May)			
W	Ezek. 34. 11–16a Ps. 23 1 Pet. 2. 19–end John 10. 11–16	Ps. 80. 1–8 Exod. 15. 1–2, 9–18 John 21. 1–19	Ps. 86 Isa. 38. 9–20 John 11. [17–26] 27–44 *or First EP of Philip and* *James* Ps. 119. 1–8 Isa. 40. 27–end John 12. 20–26 **R ct**	
	PHILIP AND JAMES, APOSTLES (transferred from 1 May)			
R	Prov. 4. 10–18 Ps. 25. 1–9 Jas. 1. [1] 2–12 John 14. 1–14	(Ps. 139; 146) Isa. 30. 1–5 John 12. 20–26	(Ps. 149) Job 23. 1–12 John 1. 43–end	
	The Invention of the Cross			
Wr		Exod. 20. 1–21 Luke 1. 26–38	Deut. 5. 22–end Eph. 1. 15–end	
W		Exod. ch. 24 Luke 1. 39–56	Deut. ch. 6 Eph. 2. 1–10	
W		Exod. 25. 1–22 Luke 1. 57–end	Deut. 7. 1–11 Eph. 2. 11–end	
	John the Evangelist, ante Portam Latinam			
W	CEG of 27 December	Exod. 28. 1–4a, 29–38 Luke 2. 1–20	Deut. 7. 12–end Eph. 3. 1–13	

		Sunday Principal Service Weekday Eucharist	Third Service Morning Prayer	Second Service Evening Prayer

7 Saturday

W		Acts 9. 31–42 Ps. 116. 10–15 John 6. 60–69	Ps. 108; *110*; 111 *alt.* Ps. 41; *42*; 43 Exod. 29. 1–9 Luke 2. 21–40	Ps. 23; *27* *alt.* Ps. 45; *46* Deut. ch. 8 Eph. 3. 14–end **ct**

8 Sunday   THE FOURTH SUNDAY OF EASTER

W	*The reading from Acts must be used as either the first or second reading at the Principal Service.*	Acts 9. 36–end [*or* Gen. 7. 1–5, 11–18; 8. 6–18; 9. 8–13] Ps. 23 Rev. 7. 9–end John 10. 22–30	Ps. 146 1 Kings 17. 17–end Luke 7. 11–23	Ps. 113; 114 Isa. 63. 7–14 Luke 24. 36–49

9 Monday

W		Acts 11. 1–18 Ps. 42. 1–2; 43. 1–4 John 10. 1–10 (*or* 11–18)	Ps. 103 *alt.* Ps. 44 Exod. 32. 1–14 Luke 2. 41–end	Ps. 112; 113; 114 *alt.* Ps. *47*; 49 Deut. 9. 1–21 Eph. 4. 1–16

10 Tuesday

W		Acts 11. 19–26 Ps. 87 John 10. 22–30	Ps. 139 *alt.* Ps. *48*; 52 Exod. 32. 15–34 Luke 3. 1–14	Ps. 115; *116* *alt.* Ps. 50 Deut. 9.23 – 10.5 Eph. 4. 17–end

11 Wednesday

W		Acts 12.24 – 13.5 Ps. 67 John 12. 44–end	Ps. 135 *alt.* Ps. 119. 57–80 Exod. ch. 33 Luke 3. 15–22	Ps. *47*; 48 *alt.* Ps. *59*; 60; (67) Deut. 10. 12–end Eph. 5. 1–14

12 Thursday   *Gregory Dix, Priest, Monk, Scholar, 1952*

W		Acts 13. 13–25 Ps. 89. 1–2, 20–26 John 13. 16–20	Ps. 118 *alt.* Ps. 56; *57*; (63†) Exod. 34. 1–10, 27–end Luke 4. 1–13	Ps. 81; *85* *alt.* Ps. 61; *62*; 64 Deut. 11. 8–end Eph. 5. 15–end

13 Friday

W		Acts 13. 26–33 Ps. 2 John 14. 1–6	Ps. 33 *alt.* Ps. *51*; 54 Exod. 35.20 – 36.7 Luke 4. 14–30	Ps. *36*; 40 *alt.* Ps. 38 Deut. 12. 1–14 Eph. 6. 1–9 *or First EP of Matthias* Ps. 147 Isa. 22. 15–22 Phil. 3.13b – 4.1 **R ct**

Calendar and Holy Communion	Morning Prayer	Evening Prayer	NOTES
W	Exod. 29. 1–9 Luke 2. 21–40	Deut. ch. 8 Eph. 3. 14–end	
		ct	
THE THIRD SUNDAY AFTER EASTER			
W Gen. 45. 3–10 Ps. 57 1 Pet. 2. 11–17 John 16. 16–22	Ps. 146 1 Kings 17. 17–end Luke 7. 11–23	Ps. 113; 114 Isa. 63. 7–14 Luke 24. 36–49	
W	Exod. 32. 1–14 Luke 2. 41–end	Deut. 9. 1–21 Eph. 4. 1–16	
W	Exod. 32. 15–34 Luke 3. 1–14	Deut. 9.23 – 10.5 Eph. 4. 17–end	
W	Exod. ch. 33 Luke 3. 15–22	Deut. 10. 12–end Eph. 5. 1–14	
W	Exod. 34. 1–10, 27–end Luke 4. 1–13	Deut. 11. 8–end Eph. 5. 15–end	
W	Exod. 35.20 – 36.7 Luke 4. 14–30	Deut. 12. 1–14 Eph. 6. 1–9	

		Sunday Principal Service Weekday Eucharist	Third Service Morning Prayer	Second Service Evening Prayer

14 Saturday   MATTHIAS THE APOSTLE*

R	Isa. 22. 15–end *or* Acts 1. 15–end Ps. 15 Acts 1. 15–end *or* 1 Cor. 4. 1–7 John 15. 9–17	*MP*: Ps. 16; 147. 1–12 1 Sam. 2. 27–35 Acts 2. 37–end	*EP*: Ps. 80 1 Sam. 16. 1–13a Matt. 7. 15–27

	or, if Matthias is celebrated on 24 February:		
W	Acts 13. 44–end Ps. 98. 1–5 John 14. 7–14	Ps. 34 *alt.* Ps. 68 Exod. 40. 17–end Luke 4. 31–37	Ps. **84**; 86 *alt.* Ps. 65; **66** Deut. 15. 1–18 Eph. 6. 10–end **ct**

15 Sunday   THE FIFTH SUNDAY OF EASTER

W	*The reading from Acts must be used as either the first or second reading at the Principal Service.* Acts 11. 1–18 [*or* Baruch 3. 9–15, 32 – 4.4 *or* Gen. 22. 1–18] Ps. 148 (*or* 148. 1–6) Rev. 21. 1–6 John 13. 31–35	Ps. 16 2 Sam. 7. 4–13 Acts 2. 14a, 22–32 [33–36]	Ps. 98 Dan. 6. [1–5] 6–23 Mark 15.46 – 16.8

16 Monday   *Caroline Chisholm, Social Reformer, 1877*

W	Acts 14. 5–18 Ps. 118. 1–3, 14–15 John 14. 21–26	Ps. 145 *alt.* Ps. 71 Num. 9. 15–end; 10. 33–end Luke 4. 38–end	Ps. 105 *alt.* Ps. **72**; 75 Deut. 16. 1–20 1 Pet. 1. 1–12

17 Tuesday

W	Acts 14. 19–end Ps. 145. 10–end John 14. 27–end	Ps. **19**; 147. 1–12 *alt.* Ps. 73 Num. 11. 1–33 Luke 5. 1–11	Ps. 96; **97** *alt.* Ps. 74 Deut. 17. 8–end 1 Pet. 1. 13–end

18 Wednesday

W	Acts 15. 1–6 Ps. 122. 1–5 John 15. 1–8	Ps. **30**; 147. 13–end *alt.* Ps. 77 Num. ch. 12 Luke 5. 12–26	Ps. 98; **99**; 100 *alt.* Ps. 119. 81–104 Deut. 18. 9–end 1 Pet. 2. 1–10

19 Thursday   Dunstan, Archbishop of Canterbury, Restorer of Monastic Life, 988

W	Com. Bishop *or* Acts 15. 7–21 *esp.* Matt. 24. 42–46 Ps. 96. 1–3, 7–10 *also* Exod. 31. 1–5 John 15. 9–11	Ps. **57**; 148 *alt.* Ps. 78. 1–39† Num. 13. 1–3, 17–end Luke 5. 27–end	Ps. 104 *alt.* Ps. 78. 40–end† Deut. ch. 19 1 Pet. 2. 11–end

20 Friday   Alcuin of York, Deacon, Abbot of Tours, 804

W	Com. Religious *or* Acts 15. 22–31 *also* Col. 3. 12–16 Ps. 57. 8–end John 4. 19–24 John 15. 12–17	Ps. **138**; 149 *alt.* Ps. 55 Num. 14. 1–25 Luke 6. 1–11	Ps. 66 *alt.* Ps. 69 Deut. 21.22 – 22.8 1 Pet. 3. 1–12

*Matthias may be celebrated on 24 February instead of 14 May.

	Calendar and Holy Communion	Morning Prayer	Evening Prayer	NOTES
W		Exod. 40. 17–end Luke 4. 31–37	Deut. 15. 1–18 Eph. 6. 10–end	
			ct	

THE FOURTH SUNDAY AFTER EASTER

	Calendar and Holy Communion	Morning Prayer	Evening Prayer	NOTES
W	Job 19. 21–27a Ps. 66. 14–end Jas. 1. 17–21 John 16. 5–15	Ps. 16 2 Sam. 7. 4–13 Acts 2. 14a, 22–32 [33–36]	Ps. 98 Dan. 6. [1–5] 6–23 Mark 15.46 – 16.8	
W		Num. 9. 15–end; 10. 33–end Luke 4. 38–end	Deut. 16. 1–20 1 Pet. 1. 1–12	
W		Num. 11. 1–33 Luke 5. 1–11	Deut. 17. 8–end 1 Pet. 1. 13–end	
W		Num. ch. 12 Luke 5. 12–26	Deut. 18. 9–end 1 Pet. 2. 1–10	

Dunstan, Archbishop of Canterbury, Restorer of Monastic Life, 988

	Calendar and Holy Communion	Morning Prayer	Evening Prayer	NOTES
W	Com. Bishop	Num. 13. 1–3, 17–end Luke 5. 27–end	Deut. ch. 19 1 Pet. 2. 11–end	
W		Num. 14. 1–25 Luke 6. 1–11	Deut. 21.22 – 22.8 1 Pet. 3. 1–12	

		Sunday Principal Service Weekday Eucharist	Third Service Morning Prayer	Second Service Evening Prayer

21 Saturday — *Helena, Protector of the Holy Places, 330*

| W | | Acts 16. 1–10
Ps. 100
John 15. 18–21 | Ps. *146*; 150
alt. Ps. *76*; 79
Num. 14. 26–end
Luke 6. 12–26 | Ps. 118
alt. Ps. 81; *84*
Deut. 24. 5–end
1 Pet. 3. 13–end
ct |

22 Sunday — **THE SIXTH SUNDAY OF EASTER**

| W | *The reading from Acts must be used as either the first or second reading at the Principal Service.* | Acts 16. 9–15
[*or* Ezek. 37. 1–14]
Ps. 67
Rev. 21.10, 22 – 22.5
John 14. 23–29
or John 5. 1–9 | Ps. 40. 1–9
Gen. 1. 26–28 [29–end]
Col. 3. 1–11 | Ps. 126; 127
Zeph. 3. 14–end
Matt. 28. 1–10, 16–end |

23 Monday — Rogation Day*

| W | | Acts 16. 11–15
Ps. 149. 1–5
John 15.26 – 16.4 | Ps. *65*; 67
alt. Ps. *80*; 82
Num. 16. 1–35
Luke 6. 27–38 | Ps. *121*; 122; 123
alt. Ps. *85*; 86
Deut. ch. 26
1 Pet. 4. 1–11 |

24 Tuesday — John and Charles Wesley, Evangelists, Hymn Writers, 1791 and 1788
Rogation Day*

| W | Com. Pastor *or*
also Eph. 5. 15–20 | Acts 16. 22–34
Ps. 138
John 16. 5–11 | Ps. 124; 125; *126*; 127
alt. Ps. 87; *89. 1–18*
Num. 16. 36–end
Luke 6. 39–end | Ps. *128*; 129; 130; 131
alt. Ps. 89. 19–end
Deut. 28. 1–14
1 Pet. 4. 12–end |

25 Wednesday — The Venerable Bede, Monk at Jarrow, Scholar, Historian, 735
Rogation Day*
Aldhelm, Bishop of Sherborne, 709

| W | Com. Religious *or*
also Ecclus. 39. 1–10 | Acts 17.15, 22 – 18.1
Ps. 148. 1–2, 11–end
John 16. 12–15 | Ps. *132*; 133
alt. Ps. 119. 105–128
Num. 17. 1–11
Luke 7. 1–10 | *First EP of Ascension Day*
Ps. 15; 24
2 Sam. 23. 1–5
Col. 2.20 – 3.4
𝔚 **ct** |

26 Thursday — **ASCENSION DAY**

| 𝔴 | *The reading from Acts must be used as either the first or second reading at the Eucharist.* | Acts 1. 1–11
or Dan. 7. 9–14
Ps. 47 *or* Ps. 93
Eph. 1. 15–end
or Acts 1. 1–11
Luke 24. 44–end | *MP*: Ps. 110; 150
Isa. 52. 7–end
Heb. 7. [11–25] 26–end | *EP*: Ps. 8
Song of the Three 29–37
or 2 Kings 2. 1–15
Rev. ch. 5
Gospel: Matt. 28. 16–end |

27 Friday

| W | | Acts 18. 9–18
Ps. 47. 1–6
John 16. 20–23 | Ps. 20; *81*
alt. Ps. *88*; (95)
Num. 20. 1–13
Luke 7. 11–17
[Exod. 35.30 – 36.1
Gal. 5. 13–end]** | Ps. 145
alt. Ps. 102
Deut. 29. 2–15
1 John 1.1 – 2.6 |

*For Rogation Day provision, see p. 11.
**The alternative readings in square brackets may be used at one of the offices, in preparation for the Day of Pentecost.

	Calendar and Holy Communion	Morning Prayer	Evening Prayer	NOTES
W		Num. 14. 26–end Luke 6. 12–26	Deut. 24. 5–end 1 Pet. 3. 13–end	
			ct	

THE FIFTH SUNDAY AFTER EASTER
Rogation Sunday

W	Joel 2. 21–26 Ps. 66. 1–8 Jas. 1. 22–end John 16. 23b–end	Ps. 40. 1–9 Gen. 1. 26–28 [29–end] John 5. 1–9	Ps. 126; 127 Zeph. 3. 14–end Matt. 28. 1–10, 16–end	
	Rogation Day			
W	Job 28. 1–11 Ps. 107. 1–9 Jas. 5. 7–11 Luke 6. 36–42	Num. 16. 1–35 Luke 6. 27–38	Deut. ch. 26 1 Pet. 4. 1–11	
	Rogation Day			
W	Deut. 8. 1–10 Ps. 121 Jas. 5. 16–end Luke 11. 5–13	Num. 16. 36–end Luke 6. 39–end	Deut. 28. 1–14 1 Pet. 4. 12–end	
	Rogation Day			
W	Deut. 34. 1–7 Ps. 108. 1–6 Eph. 4. 7–13 John 17. 1–11	Num. 17. 1–11 Luke 7. 1–10	*First EP of Ascension Day* Ps. 15; 24 2 Sam. 23. 1–5 Col. 2.20 – 3.4 𝔚 ct	

ASCENSION DAY

𝔴	Dan. 7. 13–14 Ps. 68. 1–6 Acts 1. 1–11 Mark 16. 14–end or Luke 24. 44–end	Ps. 110; 150 Isa. 52. 7–end Heb. 7. [11–25] 26–end	Ps. 8 Song of the Three 29–37 or 2 Kings 2. 1–15 Rev. ch. 5	

The Venerable Bede, Monk at Jarrow, Scholar, Historian, 735

W	Com. Religious *or* Ascension CEG	Num. 20. 1–13 Luke 7. 11–17 [Exod. 35.30 – 36.1 Gal. 5. 13–end]**	Deut. 29. 2–15 1 John 1.1 – 2.6	

		Sunday Principal Service Weekday Eucharist	Third Service Morning Prayer	Second Service Evening Prayer
28 Saturday	*Lanfranc, Prior of Le Bec, Archbishop of Canterbury, Scholar, 1089*			
W		Acts 18. 22–end Ps. 47. 1–2, 7–end John 16. 23–28	Ps. 21; ***47*** *alt.* Ps. 96; ***97***; 100 Num. 21. 4–9 Luke 7. 18–35 [Num. 11. 16–17, 24–29 1 Cor. ch. 2]*	Ps. 84; ***85*** *alt.* Ps. 104 Deut. ch. 30 1 John 2. 7–17 **ct**
29 Sunday	**THE SEVENTH SUNDAY OF EASTER (SUNDAY AFTER ASCENSION DAY)**			
W	*The reading from Acts must be used as either the first or second reading at the Principal Service.*	Acts 16. 16–34 [or Ezek. 36. 24–28] Ps. 97 Rev. 22. 12–14, 16–17, 20–end John 17. 20–end	Ps. 99 Deut. ch. 34 Luke 24. 44–end *or* Acts 1. 1–8	Ps. 68 (*or* 68. 1–13, 18–19) Isa. 44. 1–8 Eph. 4. 7–16 *Gospel*: Luke 24. 44–end
30 Monday	**Josephine Butler, Social Reformer, 1906** *Joan of Arc, Visionary, 1431; Apolo Kivebulaya, Evangelist in Central Africa, 1933*			
W	Com. Saint *or* *esp.* Isa. 58. 6–11 *also* 1 John 3. 18–23 Matt. 9. 10–13	Acts 19. 1–8 Ps. 68. 1–6 John 16. 29–end	Ps. ***93***; 96; 97 *alt.* Ps. ***98***; 99; 101 Num. 22. 1–35 Luke 7. 36–end [Num. 27. 15–end 1 Cor. ch. 3]*	Ps. 18 *alt.* Ps. ***105***† (*or* 103) Deut. 31. 1–13 1 John 2. 18–end *or First EP of the Visit of Mary to Elizabeth* Ps. 45 Song of Sol. 2. 8–14 Luke 1. 26–38 **ct**
31 Tuesday	**THE VISIT OF THE BLESSED VIRGIN MARY TO ELIZABETH**** Rogation Day***			
W		Zeph. 3. 14–18 Ps. 113 Rom. 12. 9–16 Luke 1. 39–49 [50–56]	*MP*: Ps. 85; 150 1 Sam. 2. 1–10 Mark 3. 31–end	*EP*: Ps. 122; 127; 128 Zech. 2. 10–end John 3. 25–30
	or, if The Visitation is celebrated on 2 July:			
W		Acts 20. 17–27 Ps. 68. 9–10, 18–19 John 17. 1–11	Ps. 98; ***99***; 100 *alt.* Ps. ***106***† (*or* 103) Num. 22.36 - 23.12 Luke 8. 1–15 [1 Sam. 10. 1–10 1 Cor. 12. 1–13]*	Ps. 68 *alt.* Ps. 107† Deut. 31. 14–29 1 John 3. 1–10

June 2022

1 Wednesday	**Justin, Martyr at Rome, c. 165**			
Wr	Com. Martyr *or* *esp.* John 15. 18–21 *also* 1 Macc. 2. 15–22 1 Cor. 1. 18–25	Acts 20. 28–end Ps. 68. 27–28, 32–end John 17. 11–19	Ps. 2; ***29*** *alt.* Ps. 110; ***111***; 112 Num. 23. 13–end Luke 8. 16–25 [1 Kings 19. 1–18 Matt. 3. 13–end]*	Ps. 36; ***46*** *alt.* Ps. 119. 129–152 Deut. 31.30 - 32.14 1 John 3. 11–end

*The alternative readings in square brackets may be used at one of the offices, in preparation for the Day of Pentecost.
**The Visit of the Blessed Virgin Mary to Elizabeth may be celebrated on 2 July instead of 31 May.
***For Rogation Day provision, see p. 11.

	Calendar and Holy Communion	Morning Prayer	Evening Prayer	NOTES
	Ascension CEG			
W		Num. 21. 4–9 Luke 7. 18–35 [Num. 11. 16–17, 24–29 1 Cor. ch. 2]*	Deut. ch. 30 1 John 2. 7–17	
			ct	
	THE SUNDAY AFTER ASCENSION DAY			
W	2 Kings 2. 9–15 Ps. 68. 32–end 1 Pet. 4. 7–11 John 15.26 – 16.4a	Ps. 99 Deut. ch. 34 Luke 24. 44–end or Acts 1. 1–8	Ps. 68 (or 68. 1–13, 18–19) Isa. 44. 1–8 Eph. 4. 7–16	
W		Num. 22. 1–35 Luke 7. 36–end [Num. 27. 15–end 1 Cor. ch. 3]*	Deut. 31. 1–13 1 John 2. 18–end	
W		Num. 22.36 – 23.12 Luke 8. 1–15 [1 Sam. 10. 1–10 1 Cor. 12. 1–13]*	Deut. 31. 14–29 1 John 3. 1–10	
	Nicomede, Priest and Martyr at Rome (date unknown)			
Wr	Com. Martyr	Num. 23. 13–end Luke 8. 16–25 [1 Kings 19. 1–18 Matt. 3. 13–end]*	Deut. 31.30 – 32.14 1 John 3. 11–end	

		Sunday Principal Service Weekday Eucharist	Third Service Morning Prayer	Second Service Evening Prayer
2 Thursday				
W		Acts 22. 30; 23. 6–11 Ps. 16. 1, 5–end John 17. 20–end	Ps. **24**; 72 *alt.* Ps. 113; **115** Num. ch. 24 Luke 8. 26–39 [Ezek. 11. 14–20 Matt. 9.35 – 10.20]*	Ps. 139 *alt.* Ps. 114; **116**; 117 Deut. 32. 15–47 1 John 4. 1–6
3 Friday	*The Martyrs of Uganda, 1885–87 and 1977*			
W		Acts 25. 13–21 Ps. 103. 1–2, 11–12, 19–20 John 21. 15–19	Ps. **28**; 30 *alt.* Ps. 139 Num. 27. 12–end Luke 8. 40–end [Ezek. 36. 22–28 Matt. 12. 22–32]*	Ps. 147 *alt.* Ps. **130**; 131; 137 Deut. ch. 33 1 John 4. 7–end
4 Saturday	*Petroc, Abbot of Padstow, 6th century*			
W		Acts 28. 16–20, 30–end Ps. 11. 4–end John 21. 20–end	Ps. 42; **43** *alt.* Ps. 120; **121**; 122 Num. 32. 1–27 Luke 9. 1–17 [Mic. 3. 1–8 Eph. 6. 10–20]*	*First EP of Pentecost* Ps. 48 Deut. 16. 9–15 John 7. 37–39 **R** ct
5 Sunday	**DAY OF PENTECOST (Whit Sunday)**			
R	*The reading from Acts must be used as either the first or second reading at the Principal Service.*	Acts 2. 1–21 or Gen. 11. 1–9 Ps. 104. 26–36, 37b (or 104. 26–end) Rom. 8. 14–17 or Acts 2. 1–21 John 14. 8–17 [25–27]	*MP:* Ps. 36. 5–10; 150 Isa. 40. 12–23 or Wisd. 9. 9–17 1 Cor. 2. 6–end	*EP:* Ps. 33. 1–12 Exod. 33. 7–20 2 Cor. 3. 4–end *Gospel:* John 16. 4b–15
6 Monday	*Ini Kopuria, Founder of the Melanesian Brotherhood, 1945* *Ordinary Times resumes today.*			
G **DEL 10**		1 Kings 17. 1–6 Ps. 121 Matt. 5. 1–12	Ps. 123; 124; 125; **126** Josh. ch. 1 Luke 9. 18–27	Ps. **127**; 128; 129 2 Chron. 17. 1–12 Rom. 1. 1–17
7 Tuesday				
G		1 Kings. 17. 7–16 Ps. 4 Matt. 5. 13–16	Ps. **132**; 133 Josh. ch. 2 Luke 9. 28–36	Ps. (134); **135** 2 Chron. 18. 1–27 Rom. 1. 18–end
8 Wednesday	**Thomas Ken, Bishop of Bath and Wells, Nonjuror, Hymn Writer, 1711**			
Gw	Com. Bishop *or* *esp.* 2 Cor. 4. 1–10 Matt. 24. 42–46	1 Kings 18. 20–39 Ps. 16. 1, 6–end Matt. 5. 17–19	Ps. 119. 153–end Josh. ch. 3 Luke 9. 37–50	Ps. 136 2 Chron. 18.28 – 19.end Rom. 2. 1–16
9 Thursday	**Columba, Abbot of Iona, Missionary, 597** *Ephrem of Syria, Deacon, Hymn Writer, Teacher, 373*			
G	Com. Missionary *or* *also* Titus 2. 11–end	1 Kings 18. 41–end Ps. 65. 8–end Matt. 5. 20–26	Ps. **143**; 146 Josh. 4.1 – 5.1 Luke 9. 51–end	Ps. **138**; 140; 141 2 Chron. 20. 1–23 Rom. 2. 17–end

*The alternative readings in square brackets may be used at one of the offices, in preparation for the Day of Pentecost.

	Calendar and Holy Communion	Morning Prayer	Evening Prayer	NOTES
W		Num. ch. 24 Luke 8. 26–39 [Ezek. 11. 14–20 Matt. 9.35 – 10.20]*	Deut. 32. 15–47 1 John 4. 1–6	
W		Num. 27. 12–end Luke 8. 40–end [Ezek. 36. 22–28 Matt. 12. 22–32]*	Deut. ch. 33 1 John 4. 7–end	
W		Num. 32. 1–27 Luke 9. 1–17 [Mic. 3. 1–8 Eph. 6. 10–20]*	*First EP of Whit Sunday* Ps. 48 Deut. 16. 9–15 John 7. 37–39 **R ct**	

WHIT SUNDAY

	Calendar and Holy Communion	Morning Prayer	Evening Prayer	NOTES
R	Deut. 16. 9–12 Ps. 122 Acts 2. 1–11 John 14. 15–31a	Ps. 36. 5–10; 150 Isa. 40. 12–23 *or* Wisd. 9. 9–17 1 Cor. 2. 6–end	Ps. 33. 1–12 Exod. 33. 7–20 2 Cor. 3. 4–end	

Monday in Whitsun Week

R	Acts 10. 34–end John 3. 16–21	Ezek. 11. 14–20 Acts 2. 12–36	Exod. 35.30 – 36.1 Acts 2. 37–end	

Tuesday in Whitsun Week

R	Acts 8. 14–17 John 10. 1–10	Ezek. 37. 1–14 1 Cor. 12. 1–13	2 Sam. 23. 1–5 1 Cor. 12.27 – 13.end	

Ember Day

R	Ember CEG or Acts 2. 14–21 John 6. 44–51	Josh. ch. 3 Luke 9. 37–50	2 Chron. 18.28 – 19.end Rom. 2. 1–16	
R	Acts 2. 22–25 Luke 9. 1–6	Josh. 4.1 – 5.1 Luke 9. 51–end	2 Chron. 20. 1–23 Rom. 2. 17–end	

		Sunday Principal Service Weekday Eucharist	Third Service Morning Prayer	Second Service Evening Prayer

10 Friday

G		1 Kings 19. 9, 11–16 Ps. 27. 8–16 Matt. 5. 27–32	Ps. *142*; 144 Josh. 5. 2–end Luke 10. 1–16	Ps. 145 2 Chron. 22.10 – 23.end Rom. 3. 1–20 *or First EP of Barnabas* Ps. 1; 15 Isa. 42. 5–12 Acts 14. 8–end **R ct**

11 Saturday   **BARNABAS THE APOSTLE**

R		Job 29. 11–16 *or* Acts 11. 19–end Ps. 112 Acts 11. 19–end *or* Gal. 2. 1–10 John 15. 12–17	*MP*: Ps. 100; 101; 117 Jer. 9. 23–24 Acts 4. 32–end	*First EP of Trinity Sunday* Ps. 97; 98 Isa. 40. 12–end Mark 1. 1–13 **𝖂 ct**

12 Sunday   **TRINITY SUNDAY**

𝖂		Prov. 8. 1–4, 22–31 Ps. 8 Rom. 5. 1–5 John 16. 12–15	*MP*: Ps. 29 Isa. 6. 1–8 Rev. ch. 4	*EP*: Ps. 73. 1–3, 16–end Exod. 3. 1–15 John 3. 1–17

13 Monday

G **DEL 11**		1 Kings 21. 1–16 Ps. 5. 1–5 Matt. 5. 38–42	Ps. *1*; 2; 3 Josh. 7. 1–15 Luke 10. 25–37	Ps. *4*; 7 2 Chron. 26. 1–21 Rom. 4. 1–12

14 Tuesday   *Richard Baxter, Puritan Divine, 1691*

G		1 Kings 21. 17–end Ps. 51. 1–9 Matt. 5. 43–end	Ps. *5*; 6; (8) Josh. 7. 16–end Luke 10. 38–end	Ps. 9; 10† 2 Chron. ch. 28 Rom. 4. 13–end

15 Wednesday   *Evelyn Underhill, Spiritual Writer, 1941*

G		2 Kings 2. 1, 6–14 Ps. 31. 21–end Matt. 6. 1–6, 16–18	Ps. 119. 1–32 Josh. 8. 1–29 Luke 11. 1–13	Ps. *11*; 12; 13 2 Chron. 29. 1–19 Rom. 5. 1–11 *or First EP of Corpus Christi* Ps. 110; 111 Exod. 16. 2–15 John 6. 22–35 **W ct**

16 Thursday   **DAY OF THANKSGIVING FOR HOLY COMMUNION (CORPUS CHRISTI)**
Richard, Bishop of Chichester, 1253
Joseph Butler, Bishop of Durham, Philosopher, 1752

W		Gen. 14. 18–20 Ps. 116. 10–end 1 Cor. 11. 23–26 John 6. 51–58	*MP*: Ps. 147 Deut. 8. 2–16 1 Cor. 10. 1–17	*EP*: Ps. 23; 42; 43 Prov. 9. 1–5 Luke 9. 11–17
Gw	*or, if Corpus Christi is not celebrated*: Com. Bishop *or* *also* John 21. 15–19	Ecclus. 48. 1–14 *or* Isa. 63. 7–9 Ps. 97. 1–8 Matt. 6. 7–15	Ps. 14; *15*; 16 Josh. 8. 30–end Luke 11. 14–28	Ps. 18† 2 Chron. 29. 20–end Rom. 5. 12–end

	Calendar and Holy Communion	Morning Prayer	Evening Prayer	NOTES
	Ember Day			
R	Ember CEG *or* Acts 8. 5–8 Luke 5. 17–26	Josh. 5. 2–end Luke 10. 1–16	2 Chron. 22.10 – 23.end Rom. 3. 1–20 *or First EP of Barnabas:* (Ps. 1; 15) Isa. 42. 5–12 Acts 14. 8–end **R ct**	
	BARNABAS THE APOSTLE Ember Day			
R	Job 29. 11–16 Ps. 112 Acts 11. 22–end John 15. 12–16	(Ps. 100; 101; 117) Jer. 9. 23–24 Acts 4. 32–end	*First EP of Trinity Sunday* Ps. 97; 98 Isa. 40. 12–end Mark 1. 1–13 𝖂 **ct**	
	TRINITY SUNDAY			
𝖂	Isa. 6. 1–8 Ps. 8 Rev. 4. 1–11 John 3. 1–15	Ps. 29 Prov. 8. 1–4, 22–31 Rom. 5. 1–5	Ps. 73. 1–3, 16–end Exod. 3. 1–15 Matt. 28. 16–end	
G		Josh. 7. 1–15 Luke 10. 25–37	2 Chron. 26. 1–21 Rom. 4. 1–12	
G		Josh. 7. 16–end Luke 10. 38–end	2 Chron. ch. 28 Rom. 4. 13–end	
G		Josh. 8. 1–29 Luke 11. 1–13	2 Chron. 29. 1–19 Rom. 5. 1–11	

To celebrate Corpus Christi, see *Common Worship* provision.

| G | | Josh. 8. 30–end Luke 11. 14–28 | 2 Chron. 29. 20–end Rom. 5. 12–end | |

		Sunday Principal Service Weekday Eucharist	Third Service Morning Prayer	Second Service Evening Prayer
17 Friday	*Samuel and Henrietta Barnett, Social Reformers, 1913 and 1936*			
G		2 Kings 11. 1–4, 9–18, 20 Ps. 132. 1–5, 11–13 Matt. 6. 19–23	Ps. 17; *19* Josh. 9. 3–26 Luke 11. 29–36	Ps. 22 2 Chron. ch. 30 Rom. 6. 1–14
18 Saturday	*Bernard Mizeki, Apostle of the Mashona, Martyr, 1896*			
G		2 Chron. 24. 17–25 Ps. 89. 25–33 Matt. 6. 24–end	Ps. 20; 21; *23* Josh. 10. 1–15 Luke 11. 37–end	Ps. *24*; 25 2 Chron. 32. 1–22 Rom. 6. 15–end **ct**
19 Sunday	**THE FIRST SUNDAY AFTER TRINITY (Proper 7)**			
G		*Track 1* 1 Kings 19. 1–4 [5–7] 8–15a Ps. 42; 43 (or Ps. 42 or 43) Gal. 3. 23–end Luke 8. 26–39	*Track 2* Isa. 65. 1–9 Ps. 22. 19–28 Gal. 3. 23–end Luke 8. 26–39	Ps. 55. 1–16, 18–21 Deut. 11. 1–15 Acts 27. 1–12	Ps. [50]; 57 Gen. 24. 1–27 Mark 5. 21–end
20 Monday				
G **DEL 12**		2 Kings 17. 5–8, 13–15, 18 Ps. 60. 1–5, 11–end Matt. 7. 1–5	Ps. 27; *30* Josh. ch. 14 Luke 12. 1–12	Ps. 26; *28*; 29 2 Chron. 33. 1–13 Rom. 7. 1–6
21 Tuesday				
G		2 Kings 19. 9b–11, 14–21, 31–36 Ps. 48. 1–2, 8–end Matt. 7. 6, 12–14	Ps. 32; *36* Josh. 21.43 – 22.8 Luke 12. 13–21	Ps. 33 2 Chron. 34. 1–18 Rom. 7. 7–end
22 Wednesday	**Alban, first Martyr of Britain, c. 250** Ember Day*			
Gr *or* **R**	Com. Martyr *or* *esp.* 2 Tim. 2. 3–13 John 12. 24–26	2 Kings 22. 8–13; 23. 1–3 Ps. 119. 33–40 Matt. 7. 15–20	Ps. 34 Josh. 22. 9–end Luke 12. 22–31	Ps. 119. 33–56 2 Chron. 34. 19–end Rom. 8. 1–11
23 Thursday	**Etheldreda, Abbess of Ely, c. 678**			
Gw	Com. Religious *or* *also* Matt. 25. 1–13	2 Kings 24. 8–17 Ps. 79. 1–9, 12 Matt. 7. 21–end	Ps. 37† Josh. ch. 23 Luke 12. 32–40	Ps. 39; *40* 2 Chron. 35. 1–19 Rom. 8. 12–17 *or First EP of The Birth of John the Baptist* Ps. 71 Judg. 13. 2–7, 24–end Luke 1. 5–25 **W ct**
24 Friday	**THE BIRTH OF JOHN THE BAPTIST** Ember Day*			
W		Isa. 40. 1–11 Ps. 85. 7–end Acts 13. 14b–26 *or* Gal. 3. 23–end Luke 1. 57–66, 80	*MP*: Ps. 50; 149 Ecclus. 48. 1–10 *or* Mal. 3. 1–6 Luke 3. 1–17	*EP*: Ps. 80; 82 Mal. ch. 4 Matt. 11. 2–19

*For Ember Day provision, see p. 11.

	Calendar and Holy Communion	Morning Prayer	Evening Prayer	NOTES
	Alban, first Martyr of Britain, c. 250			
Gr	Com. Martyr	Josh. 9. 3–26 Luke 11. 29–36	2 Chron. ch. 30 Rom. 6. 1–14	
G		Josh. 10. 1–15 Luke 11. 37–end	2 Chron. 32. 1–22 Rom. 6. 15–end	
			ct	
	THE FIRST SUNDAY AFTER TRINITY			
G	2 Sam. 9. 6–end Ps. 41. 1–4 1 John 4. 7–end Luke 16. 19–31	Ps. 52; 53 Deut. 11. 1–15 Acts 27. 1–12	Ps. [50]; 57 Gen. 24. 1–27 Mark 5. 21–end	
	Translation of Edward, King of the West Saxons, 979			
Gr	Com. Martyr	Josh. ch. 14 Luke 12. 1–12	2 Chron. 33. 1–13 Rom. 7. 1–6	
G		Josh. 21.43 – 22.8 Luke 12. 13–21	2 Chron. 34. 1–18 Rom. 7. 7–end	
G		Josh. 22. 9–end Luke 12. 22–31	2 Chron. 34. 19–end Rom. 8. 1–11	
G		Josh. ch. 23 Luke 12. 32–40	2 Chron. 35. 1–19 Rom. 8. 12–17 *or First EP of The Birth of John the Baptist* (Ps. 71) Judg. 13. 2–7, 24–end Luke 1. 5–25	
			W ct	
	THE NATIVITY OF JOHN THE BAPTIST			
W	Isa. 40. 1–11 Ps. 80. 1–7 Acts 13. 22–26 Luke 1. 57–80	(Ps. 50; 149) Ecclus. 48. 1–10 *or* Mal. 3. 1–6 Luke 3. 1–17	(Ps. 82) Mal. ch. 4 Matt. 11. 2–19	

		Sunday Principal Service Weekday Eucharist	Third Service Morning Prayer	Second Service Evening Prayer
25 Saturday	Ember Day*			
G *or* **R**		Lam. 2. 2, 10–14, 18–19 Ps. 74. 1–3, 21–end Matt. 8. 5–17	Ps. 41; ***42***; 43 Josh. 24. 29–end Luke 12. 49–end	Ps. 45; ***46*** 2 Chron. 36. 11–end Rom. 8. 31–end **ct**
26 Sunday	**THE SECOND SUNDAY AFTER TRINITY (Proper 8)**			
G	*Track 1* 2 Kings 2. 1–2, 6–14 Ps. 77. 1–2, 11–end (*or* 77. 11–end) Gal. 5. 1, 13–25 Luke 9. 51–end	*Track 2* 1 Kings 19. 15–16, 19–end Ps. 16 Gal. 5. 1, 13–25 Luke 9. 51–end	Ps. 64 Deut. 15. 1–11 Acts 27. [13–32] 33–end	Ps. [59. 1–6, 18–end]; 60 Gen. 27. 1–40 Mark 6. 1–6
27 Monday	*Cyril, Bishop of Alexandria, Teacher, 444*			
G **DEL 13**		Amos 2. 6–10, 13–end Ps. 50. 16–23 Matt. 8. 18–22	Ps. 44 Judg. ch. 2 Luke 13. 1–9	Ps. ***47***; 49 Ezra ch. 1 Rom. 9. 1–18
28 Tuesday	**Irenaeus, Bishop of Lyons, Teacher, *c.* 200**			
Gw	Com. Teacher *or* *also* 2 Pet. 1. 16–21	Amos 3. 1–8; 4. 11–12 Ps. 5. 8–end Matt. 8. 23–27	Ps. ***48***; 52 Judg. 4. 1–23 Luke 13. 10–21	Ps. 50 Ezra ch. 3 Rom. 9. 19–end *or First EP of Peter and Paul* Ps. 66; 67 Ezek. 3. 4–11 Gal. 1.13 – 2.8 *or, for Peter alone*: Acts 9. 32–end **R ct**
29 Wednesday	**PETER AND PAUL, APOSTLES**			
R		Zech. 4. 1–6a, 10b–end *or* Acts 12. 1–11 Ps. 125 Acts 12. 1–11 *or* 2 Tim. 4. 6–8, 17–18 Matt. 16. 13–19	*MP*: Ps. 71; 113 Isa. 49. 1–6 Acts 11. 1–18	*EP*: Ps. 124; 138 Ezek. 34. 11–16 John 21. 15–22
	or, if Peter is commemorated alone:			
R		Ezek. 3. 22–end *or* Acts 12. 1–11 Ps. 125 Acts 12. 1–11 *or* 1 Pet. 2. 19–end Matt. 16. 13–19	*MP*: Ps. 71; 113 Isa. 49. 1–6 Acts 11. 1–18	*EP*: Ps. 124; 138 Ezek. 34. 11–16 John 21. 15–22
30 Thursday				
G		Amos 7. 10–end Ps. 19. 7–10 Matt. 9. 1–8	Ps. 56; ***57***; (63†) Judg. 6. 1–24 Luke 14. 1–11	Ps. 61; ***62***; 64 Ezra 4. 7–end Rom. 10. 11–end

July 2022

1 Friday	*Henry, John and Henry Venn the Younger, Priests, Evangelical Divines, 1797, 1813 and 1873*			
G		Amos 8. 4–6, 9–12 Ps. 119. 1–8 Matt. 9. 9–13	Ps. ***51***; 54 Judg. 6. 25–end Luke 14. 12–24	Ps. 38 Ezra ch. 5 Rom. 11. 1–12

*For Ember Day provision, see p. 11.

	Calendar and Holy Communion	Morning Prayer	Evening Prayer	NOTES
G		Josh. 24. 29–end Luke 12. 49–end	2 Chron. 36. 11–end Rom. 8. 31–end	
			ct	
	THE SECOND SUNDAY AFTER TRINITY			
G	Gen. 12. 1–4 Ps. 120 1 John 3. 13–end Luke 14. 16–24	Ps. 64 Deut. 15. 1–11 Acts 27. [13–32] 33–end	Ps. [59. 1–6, 18–end]; 60 Gen. 27. 1–40 Mark 6. 1–6	
G		Judg. ch. 2 Luke 13. 1–9	Ezra ch. 1 Rom. 9. 1–18	
G		Judg. 4. 1–23 Luke 13. 10–21	Ezra ch. 3 Rom. 9. 19–end *or First EP of Peter* (Ps. 66; 67) Ezek. 3. 4–11 Acts 9. 32–end	
			R ct	
	PETER THE APOSTLE			
R	Ezek. 3. 4–11 Ps. 125 Acts 12. 1–11 Matt. 16. 13–19	(Ps. 71; 113) Isa. 49. 1–6 Acts 11. 1–18	(Ps. 124; 138) Ezek. 34. 11–16 John 21. 15–22	
G		Judg. 6. 1–24 Luke 14. 1–11	Ezra 4. 7–end Rom. 10. 11–end	
G		Judg. 6. 25–end Luke 14. 12–24	Ezra ch. 5 Rom. 11. 1–12	

		Sunday Principal Service Weekday Eucharist	Third Service Morning Prayer	Second Service Evening Prayer
2 Saturday				
G		Amos 9. 11–end Ps. 85. 8–end Matt. 9. 14–17	Ps. 68 Judg. ch. 7 Luke 14. 25–end	Ps. 65; ***66*** Ezra ch. 6 Rom. 11. 13–24 **ct** *or First EP of Thomas* Ps. 27 Isa. ch. 35 Heb. 10.35 – 11.1 **R ct**
3 Sunday	**THOMAS THE APOSTLE** (or transferred to 4 July)**			
R		Hab. 2. 1–4 Ps. 31. 1–6 Eph. 2. 19–end John 20. 24–29	*MP*: Ps. 92; 146 2 Sam. 15. 17–21 *or* Ecclus. ch. 2 John 11. 1–16	*EP*: Ps. 139 Job 42. 1–6 1 Pet. 1. 3–12
	or, for The Third Sunday after Trinity (Proper 9):			
G	*Track 1* 2 Kings 5. 1–14 Ps. 30 Gal. 6. [1–6] 7–16 Luke 10. 1–11, 16–20	*Track 2* Isa. 66. 10–14 Ps. 66. 1–8 Gal. 6. [1–6] 7–16 Luke 10. 1–11, 16–20	Ps. 74 Deut. 24. 10–end Acts 28. 1–16	Ps. 65; [70] Gen. 29. 1–20 Mark 6. 7–29
4 Monday				
G **DEL 14**		Hos. 2. 14–16, 19–20 Ps. 145. 2–9 Matt. 9. 18–26	Ps. 71 Judg. 8. 22–end Luke 15. 1–10	Ps. ***72***; 75 Ezra ch. 7 Rom. 11. 25–end
5 Tuesday				
G		Hos. 8. 4–7, 11–13 Ps. 103. 8–12 Matt. 9. 32–end	Ps. 73 Judg. 9. 1–21 Luke 15. 11–end	Ps. 74 Ezra 8. 15–end Rom. 12. 1–8
6 Wednesday	*Thomas More, Scholar, and John Fisher, Bishop of Rochester, Reformation Martyrs, 1535*			
G		Hos. 10. 1–3, 7–8, 12 Ps. 115. 3–10 Matt. 10. 1–7	Ps. 77 Judg. 9. 22–end Luke 16. 1–18	Ps. 119. 81–104 Ezra ch. 9 Rom. 12. 9–end
7 Thursday				
G	***	Hos. 11. 1, 3–4, 8–9 Ps. 105. 1–7 Matt. 10. 7–15	Ps. 78. 1–39† Judg. 11. 1–11 Luke 16. 19–end	Ps. 78. 40–end† Ezra 10. 1–17 Rom. 13. 1–7
8 Friday				
G		Hos. 14. 2–end Ps. 80. 1–7 Matt. 10. 16–23	Ps. 55 Judg. 11. 29–end Luke 17. 1–10	Ps. 69 Neh. ch. 1 Rom. 13. 8–end
9 Saturday				
G		Isa. 6. 1–8 Ps. 51. 1–7 Matt. 10. 24–33	Ps. ***76***; 79 Judg. 12. 1–7 Luke 17. 11–19	Ps. 81; ***84*** Neh. ch. 2 Rom. 14. 1–12 **ct**

**Common Worship* Morning and Evening Prayer provision for 31 May may be used.
**Thomas the Apostle may be celebrated on 21 December instead of 3 July.
***Thomas Becket may be celebrated on 7 July instead of 29 December.

	Calendar and Holy Communion	Morning Prayer	Evening Prayer	NOTES
	The Visitation of the Blessed Virgin Mary*			
Gw	1 Sam. 2. 1–3 Ps. 113 Gal. 4. 1–5 Luke 1. 39–45	Judg. ch. 7 Luke 14. 25–end	Ezra ch. 6 Rom. 11. 13–24	
			ct	
	THE THIRD SUNDAY AFTER TRINITY			
G	2 Chron. 33. 9–13 Ps. 55. 17–23 1 Pet. 5. 5b–11 Luke 15. 1–10	Ps. 73 Deut. 24. 10–end Acts 28. 1–16	Ps. 65; [70] Gen. 29. 1–20 Mark 6. 7–29	
	Translation of Martin, Bishop of Tours, c. 397			
Gw	Com. Bishop	Judg. 8. 22–end Luke 15. 1–10	Ezra ch. 7 Rom. 11. 25–end	
G		Judg. 9. 1–21 Luke 15. 11–end	Ezra 8. 15–end Rom. 12. 1–8	
G		Judg. 9. 22–end Luke 16. 1–18	Ezra ch. 9 Rom. 12. 9–end	
G		Judg. 11. 1–11 Luke 16. 19–end	Ezra 10. 1–17 Rom. 13. 1–7	
G		Judg. 11. 29–end Luke 17. 1–10	Neh. ch. 1 Rom. 13. 8–end	
G		Judg. 12. 1–7 Luke 17. 11–19	Neh. ch. 2 Rom. 14. 1–12	
			ct	

		Sunday Principal Service Weekday Eucharist	Third Service Morning Prayer	Second Service Evening Prayer

10 Sunday   THE FOURTH SUNDAY AFTER TRINITY (Proper 10)

G	*Track 1* Amos 7. 7–end Ps. 82 Col. 1. 1–14 Luke 10. 25–37	*Track 2* Deut. 30. 9–14 Ps. 25. 1–10 Col. 1. 1–14 Luke 10. 25–37	Ps. 76 Deut. 28. 1–14 Acts 28. 17–end	Ps. 77 (*or* 77. 1–12) Gen. 32. 9–30 Mark 7. 1–23

11 Monday   Benedict of Nursia, Abbot of Monte Casino, Father of Western Monasticism, *c.* 550

Gw **DEL 15**	Com. Religious *or* *also* 1 Cor. 3. 10–11 Luke 18. 18–22	Isa. 1. 11–17 Ps. 50. 7–15 Matt. 10.34 – 11.1	Ps. *80*; 82 Judg. 13. 1–24 Luke 17. 20–end	Ps. *85*; 86 Neh. ch. 4 Rom. 14. 13–end

12 Tuesday

G		Isa. 7. 1–9 Ps. 48. 1–7 Matt. 11. 20–24	Ps. 87; *89. 1–18* Judg. ch. 14 Luke 18. 1–14	Ps. 89. 19–end Neh. ch. 5 Rom. 15. 1–13

13 Wednesday

G		Isa. 10. 5–7, 13–16 Ps. 94. 5–11 Matt. 11. 25–27	Ps. 119. 105–128 Judg. 15.1 – 16.3 Luke 18. 15–30	Ps. *91*; 93 Neh. 6.1 – 7.4 Rom. 15. 14–21

14 Thursday   John Keble, Priest, Tractarian, Poet, 1866

Gw	Com. Pastor *or* *also* Lam. 3. 19–26 Matt. 5. 1–8	Isa. 26. 7–9, 16–19 Ps. 102. 14–21 Matt. 11. 28–end	Ps. 90; *92* Judg. 16. 4–end Luke 18. 31–end	Ps. 94 Neh. 7.73b – 8.end Rom. 15. 22–end

15 Friday   Swithun, Bishop of Winchester, *c.* 862
               Bonaventure, Friar, Bishop, Teacher, 1274

Gw	Com. Bishop *or* *also* Jas. 5. 7–11, 13–18	Isa. 38. 1–6, 21–22, 7–8 *Canticle*: Isa. 38. 10–16 *or* Ps. 32. 1–8 Matt. 12. 1–8	Ps. *88*; (95) Judg. ch. 17 Luke 19. 1–10	Ps. 102 Neh. 9. 1–23 Rom. 16. 1–16

16 Saturday   Osmund, Bishop of Salisbury, 1099

G		Mic. 2. 1–5 Ps. 10. 1–5a, 12 Matt. 12. 14–21	Ps. 96; *97*; 100 Judg. 18. 1–20, 27–end Luke 19. 11–27	Ps. 104 Neh. 9. 24–end Rom. 16. 17–end ct

17 Sunday   THE FIFTH SUNDAY AFTER TRINITY (Proper 11)

G	*Track 1* Amos 8. 1–12 Ps. 52 Col. 1. 15–28 Luke 10. 38–end	*Track 2* Gen. 18. 1–10a Ps. 15 Col. 1. 15–28 Luke 10. 38–end	Ps. 82; 100 Deut. 30. 1–10 1 Pet. 3. 8–18	Ps. 81 Gen. 41. 1–16, 25–37 1 Cor. 4. 8–13 *Gospel*: John 4. 31–35

18 Monday   Elizabeth Ferard, first Deaconess of the Church of England, Founder of the Community of St Andrew, 1883

G **DEL 16**		Mic. 6. 1–4, 6–8 Ps. 50. 3–7, 14 Matt. 12. 38–42	Ps. *98*; 99; 101 1 Sam. 1. 1–20 Luke 19. 28–40	Ps. *105*† (*or* 103) Neh. 12. 27–47 2 Cor. 1. 1–14

19 Tuesday   Gregory, Bishop of Nyssa, and his sister Macrina, Deaconess, Teachers, *c.* 394 and *c.* 379

Gw	Com. Teacher *esp.* 1 Cor. 2. 9–13 *also* Wisd. 9. 13–17	Mic. 7. 14–15, 18–20 Ps. 85. 1–7 Matt. 12. 46–end	Ps. *106*† (*or* 103) 1 Sam. 1.21 – 2.11 Luke 19. 41–end	Ps. 107† Neh. 13. 1–14 2 Cor. 1.15 – 2.4

	Calendar and Holy Communion	Morning Prayer	Evening Prayer	NOTES
	THE FOURTH SUNDAY AFTER TRINITY			
G	Gen. 3. 17–19 Ps. 79. 8–10 Rom. 8. 18–23 Luke 6. 36–42	Ps. 76 Deut. 28. 1–14 Acts 28. 17–end	Ps. 77 (or 77. 1–12) Gen. 32. 9–30 Mark 7. 1–23	
G		Judg. 13. 1–24 Luke 17. 20–end	Neh. ch. 4 Rom. 14. 13–end	
G		Judg. ch. 14 Luke 18. 1–14	Neh. ch. 5 Rom. 15. 1–13	
G		Judg. 15.1 – 16.3 Luke 18. 15–30	Neh. 6.1 – 7.4 Rom. 15. 14–21	
G		Judg. 16. 4–end Luke 18. 31–end	Neh. 7.73b – 8.end Rom. 15. 22–end	
	Swithun, Bishop of Winchester, c. 862			
Gw	Com. Bishop	Judg. ch. 17 Luke 19. 1–10	Neh. 9. 1–23 Rom. 16. 1–16	
G		Judg. 18. 1–20, 27–end Luke 19. 11–27	Neh. 9. 24–end Rom. 16. 17–end	
			ct	
	THE FIFTH SUNDAY AFTER TRINITY			
G	1 Kings 19. 19–21 Ps. 84. 8–end 1 Pet. 3. 8–15a Luke 5. 1–11	Ps. 82; 100 Deut. 30. 1–10 1 Pet. 3. 8–18	Ps. 81 Gen. 41. 1–16, 25–37 1 Cor. 4. 8–13	
G		1 Sam. 1. 1–20 Luke 19. 28–40	Neh. 12. 27–47 2 Cor. 1. 1–14	
G		1 Sam. 1.21 – 2.11 Luke 19. 41–end	Neh. 13. 1–14 2 Cor. 1.15 – 2.4	

		Sunday Principal Service Weekday Eucharist	Third Service Morning Prayer	Second Service Evening Prayer
20 Wednesday	*Margaret of Antioch, Martyr, 4th century; Bartolomé de las Casas, Apostle to the Indies, 1566*			
G		Jer. 1. 1, 4–10 Ps. 70 Matt. 13. 1–9	Ps, 110; ***111***; 112 1 Sam. 2. 12–26 Luke 20. 1–8	Ps. 119. 129–152 Neh. 13. 15–end 2 Cor. 2. 5–end
21 Thursday				
G		Jer. 2. 1–3, 7–8, 12–13 Ps. 36. 5–10 Matt. 13. 10–17	Ps. 113; ***115*** 1 Sam. 2. 27–end Luke 20. 9–19	Ps. 114; ***116***; 117 Esther ch. 1 2 Cor. ch. 3 *or First EP of Mary Magdalene* Ps. 139 Isa. 25. 1–9 2 Cor. 1. 3–7 **W ct**
22 Friday	**MARY MAGDALENE**			
W		Song of Sol. 3. 1–4 Ps. 42. 1–10 2 Cor. 5. 14–17 John 20. 1–2, 11–18	*MP*: Ps. 30; 32; 150 1 Sam. 16. 14–end Luke 8. 1–3	*EP*: Ps. 63 Zeph. 3. 14–end Mark 15.40 – 16.7
23 Saturday	*Bridget of Sweden, Abbess of Vadstena, 1373*			
G		Jer. 7. 1–11 Ps. 84. 1–6 Matt. 13. 24–30	Ps. 120; ***121***; 122 1 Sam. 4. 1b–end Luke 20. 27–40	Ps. 118 Esther ch. 3 2 Cor. ch. 5 **ct**
24 Sunday	**THE SIXTH SUNDAY AFTER TRINITY (Proper 12)**			
G	*Track 1* Hos. 1. 2–10 Ps. 85 (*or* 85. 1–7) Col. 2. 6–15 [16–19] Luke 11. 1–13	*Track 2* Gen. 18. 20–32 Ps. 138 Col. 2. 6–15 [16–19] Luke 11. 1–13	Ps. 95 Song of Sol. ch. 2 *or* 1 Macc. 2. [1–14] 15–22 1 Pet. 4. 7–14	Ps. 88 (*or* 88. 1–10) Gen. 42. 1–25 1 Cor. 10. 1–24 *Gospel*: Matt. 13. 24–30 [31–43] *or First EP of James* Ps. 144 Deut. 30. 11–end Mark 5. 21–end **R ct**
25 Monday	**JAMES THE APOSTLE**			
R **DEL 17**		Jer. 45. 1–5 *or* Acts 11.27 – 12.2 Ps. 126 Acts 11.27 – 12.2 *or* 2 Cor. 4. 7–15 Matt. 20. 20–28	*MP*: Ps. 7; 29; 117 2 Kings 1. 9–15 Luke 9. 46–56	*EP*: Ps. 94 Jer. 26. 1–15 Mark 1. 14–20
26 Tuesday	**Anne and Joachim, Parents of the Blessed Virgin Mary**			
Gw	Zeph. 3. 14–18a Ps. 127 Rom. 8. 28–30 Matt. 13. 16–17	*or* Jer. 14. 17–end Ps. 79. 8–end Matt. 13. 36–43	Ps. ***132***; 133 1 Sam. 6. 1–16 Luke 21. 5–19	Ps. (134); ***135*** Esther ch. 5 2 Cor. 7. 2–end
27 Wednesday	*Brooke Foss Westcott, Bishop of Durham, Teacher, 1901*			
G		Jer. 15. 10, 16–end Ps. 59. 1–4, 18–end Matt. 13. 44–46	Ps. 119. 153–end 1 Sam. ch. 7 Luke 21. 20–28	Ps. 136 Esther 6. 1–13 2 Cor. 8. 1–15

	Calendar and Holy Communion	Morning Prayer	Evening Prayer	NOTES
	Margaret of Antioch, Martyr, 4th century			
Gr	Com. Virgin Martyr	1 Sam. 2. 12–26 Luke 20. 1–8	Neh. 13. 15–end 2 Cor. 2. 5–end	
G		1 Sam. 2. 27–end Luke 20. 9–19	Esther ch. 1 2 Cor. ch. 3 *or First EP of Mary Magdalene* (Ps. 139) Isa. 25. 1–9 2 Cor. 1. 3–7	
			W ct	
	MARY MAGDALENE			
W	Zeph. 3. 14–end Ps. 30. 1–5 2 Cor. 5. 14–17 John 20. 11–18	(Ps. 30; 32; 150) 1 Sam. 16. 14–end Luke 8. 1–3	(Ps. 63) Song of Sol. 3. 1–4 Mark 15.40 – 16.7	
G		1 Sam. 4. 1b–end Luke 20. 27–40	Esther ch. 3 2 Cor. ch. 5	
			ct	
	THE SIXTH SUNDAY AFTER TRINITY			
G	Gen. 4. 2b–15 Ps. 90. 12–end Rom. 6. 3–11 Matt. 5. 20–26	Ps. 96 Song of Sol. ch. 2 *or 1 Macc. 2. [1–14]* 15–22 1 Pet. 4. 7–14	Ps. 88 (*or* 88. 1–10) Gen. 42. 1–25 1 Cor. 9. 16–end *or First EP of James* Ps. 144 Deut. 30. 11–end Mark 5. 21–end	
			R ct	
	JAMES THE APOSTLE			
R	2 Kings 1. 9–15 Ps. 15 Acts 11.27 – 12.3a Matt. 20. 20–28	(Ps. 7; 29; 117) Jer. 45. 1–5 Luke 9. 46–56	(Ps. 94) Jer. 26. 1–15 Mark 1. 14–20	
	Anne, Mother of the Blessed Virgin Mary			
Gw	Com. Saint	1 Sam. 6. 1–16 Luke 21. 5–19	Esther ch. 5 2 Cor. 7. 2–end	
G		1 Sam. ch. 7 Luke 21. 20–28	Esther 6. 1–13 2 Cor. 8. 1–15	

		Sunday Principal Service Weekday Eucharist	Third Service Morning Prayer	Second Service Evening Prayer
28 Thursday				
G		Jer. 18. 1–6 Ps. 146. 1–5 Matt. 13. 47–53	Ps. *143*; 146 1 Sam. ch. 8 Luke 21. 29–end	Ps. *138*; 140; 141 Esther 6.14 – 7.end 2 Cor. 8.16 – 9.5
29 Friday	Mary, Martha and Lazarus, Companions of Our Lord			
Gw	Isa. 25. 6–9 *or* Ps. 49. 1–10, 16 Heb. 2. 10–15 John 12. 1–8	Jer. 26. 1–9 Ps. 69. 4–10 Matt. 13. 54–end	Ps. 142; *144* 1 Sam. 9. 1–14 Luke 22. 1–13	Ps. 145 Esther ch. 8 2 Cor. 9. 6–end
30 Saturday	William Wilberforce, Social Reformer, Olaudah Equiano and Thomas Clarkson, Anti-Slavery Campaigners, 1833, 1797 and 1846			
Gw	Com. Saint *or* *also* Job 31. 16–23 Gal. 3. 26–end; 4. 6–7 Luke 4. 16–21	Jer. 26. 11–16, 24 Ps. 69. 14–20 Matt. 14. 1–12	Ps. 147 1 Sam. 9.15 – 10.1 Luke 22. 14–23	Ps. *148*; 149; 150 Esther 9. 20–28 2 Cor. ch. 10 ct
31 Sunday	THE SEVENTH SUNDAY AFTER TRINITY (Proper 13)			
G	*Track 1* Hos. 11. 1–11 Ps. 107. 1–9, 43 (*or* 107. 1–9) Col. 3. 1–11 Luke 12. 13–21	*Track 2* Eccles. 1. 2, 12–14; 2. 18–23 Ps. 49. 1–12 (*or* 49. 1–9) Col. 3. 1–11 Luke 12. 13–21	Ps. 106. 1–10 Song of Sol. 5. 2–end *or* 1 Macc. 3. 1–12 2 Pet. 1. 1–15	Ps. 107. 1–32 (*or* 107. 1–12) Gen. 50. 4–end 1 Cor. 14. 1–19 *Gospel:* Mark 6. 45–52

August 2022

		Sunday Principal Service Weekday Eucharist	Third Service Morning Prayer	Second Service Evening Prayer
1 Monday				
G **DEL 18**		Jer. ch. 28 Ps. 119. 89–96 Matt. 14. 13–21 (*or* 14. 22–end)	Ps. *1*; 2; 3 1 Sam. 10. 1–16 Luke 22. 24–30	Ps. *4*; 7 Jer. ch. 26 2 Cor. 11. 1–15
2 Tuesday				
G		Jer. 30. 1–2, 12–15, 18–22 Ps. 102. 16–21 Matt. 14. 22–end *or* 15. 1–2, 10–14	Ps. *5*; 6; (8) 1 Sam. 10. 17–end Luke 22. 31–38	Ps. *9*; 10† Jer. ch. 28 2 Cor. 11. 16–end
3 Wednesday				
G		Jer. 31. 1–7 Ps. 121 Matt. 15. 21–28	Ps. 119. 1–32 1 Sam. ch. 11 Luke 22. 39–46	Ps. *11*; 12; 13 Jer. 29. 1–14 2 Cor. ch. 12
4 Thursday	John-Baptiste Vianney, Curé d'Ars, Spiritual Guide, 1859			
G		Jer. 31. 31–34 Ps. 51. 11–18 Matt. 16. 13–23	Ps. 14; *15*; 16 1 Sam. ch. 12 Luke 22. 47–62	Ps. 18† Jer. 30. 1–11 2 Cor. ch. 13
5 Friday	Oswald, King of Northumbria, Martyr, 642			
Gr	Com. Martyr *or* *esp.* 1 Pet. 4. 12–end John 16. 29–end	Nahum 2. 1, 3; 3. 1–3, 6–7 Ps. 137. 1–6 *or* Deut. 32. 35–36, 39, 41 Matt. 16. 24–28	Ps. 17; *19* 1 Sam. 13. 5–18 Luke 22. 63–end	Ps. 22 Jer. 30. 12–22 Jas. 1. 1–11 *or First EP of The* *Transfiguration* Ps. 99; 110 Exod. 24. 12–end John 12. 27–36a 𝔚 ct

	Calendar and Holy Communion	Morning Prayer	Evening Prayer	NOTES
G		1 Sam. ch. 8 Luke 21. 29–end	Esther 6.14 – 7.end 2 Cor. 8.16 – 9.5	
G		1 Sam. 9. 1–14 Luke 22. 1–13	Esther ch. 8 2 Cor. 9. 6–end	
G		1 Sam. 9.15 – 10.1 Luke 22. 14–23	Esther 9. 20–28 2 Cor. ch. 10 ct	

THE SEVENTH SUNDAY AFTER TRINITY

	Calendar and Holy Communion	Morning Prayer	Evening Prayer	NOTES
G	1 Kings 17. 8–16 Ps. 34. 11–end Rom. 6. 19–end Mark 8. 1–10a	Ps. 106. 1–10 Song of Sol. 5. 2–end or 1 Macc. 3. 1–12 2 Pet. 1. 1–15	Ps. 107. 1–32 (or 107. 1–12) Gen. 50. 4–end 1 Cor. 14. 1–19	

	Lammas Day			
G		1 Sam. 10. 1–16 Luke 22. 24–30	Jer. ch. 26 2 Cor. 11. 1–15	
G		1 Sam. 10. 17–end Luke 22. 31–38	Jer. ch. 28 2 Cor. 11. 16–end	
G		1 Sam. ch. 11 Luke 22. 39–46	Jer. 29. 1–14 2 Cor. ch. 12	
G		1 Sam. ch. 12 Luke 22. 47–62	Jer. 30. 1–11 2 Cor. ch. 13	
G		1 Sam. 13. 5–18 Luke 22. 63–end	Jer. 30. 12–22 Jas. 1. 1–11 or First EP of The Transfiguration (Ps. 99; 110) Exod. 24. 12–end John 12. 27–36a 𝖂 ct	

		Sunday Principal Service Weekday Eucharist	Third Service Morning Prayer	Second Service Evening Prayer
6 Saturday	**THE TRANSFIGURATION OF OUR LORD**			
﷠		Dan. 7. 9–10, 13–14 Ps. 97 2 Pet. 1. 16–19 Luke 9. 28–36	*MP*: Ps. 27; 150 Ecclus. 48. 1–10 *or* 1 Kings 19. 1–16 1 John 3. 1–3	*EP*: Ps. 72 Exod. 34. 29–end 2 Cor. ch. 3
7 Sunday	**THE EIGHTH SUNDAY AFTER TRINITY (Proper 14)**			
G	*Track 1* Isa. 1. 1, 10–20 Ps. 50. 1–8, 23–end (*or* 50. 1–7) Heb. 11. 1–3, 8–16 Luke 12. 32–40	*Track 2* Gen. 15. 1–6 Ps. 33. 12–end (*or* 33. 12–21) Heb. 11. 1–3, 8–16 Luke 12. 32–40	Ps. 115 Song of Sol. 8. 5–7 *or* 1 Macc. 14. 4–15 2 Pet. 3. 8–13	Ps. 108; [116] Isa. 11.10 – 12.end 2 Cor. 1. 1–22 *Gospel*: Mark 7. 24–30
8 Monday	**Dominic, Priest, Founder of the Order of Preachers, 1221**			
Gw **DEL 19**	Com. Religious *or* *also* Ecclus. 39. 1–10	Ezek. 1. 2–5, 24–end Ps. 148. 1–4, 12–13 Matt. 17. 22–end	Ps. 27; *30* 1 Sam. 14. 24–46 Luke 23. 13–25	Ps. 26; *28*; 29 Jer. 31. 23–25, 27–37 Jas. 2. 1–13
9 Tuesday	**Mary Sumner, Founder of the Mothers' Union, 1921**			
Gw	Com. Saint *or* *also* Heb. 13. 1–5	Ezek. 2.8 – 3.4 Ps. 119. 65–72 Matt. 18. 1–5, 10, 12–14	Ps. 32; *36* 1 Sam. 15. 1–23 Luke 23. 26–43	Ps. 33 Jer. 32. 1–15 Jas. 2. 14–end
10 Wednesday	**Laurence, Deacon at Rome, Martyr, 258**			
Gr	Com. Martyr *or* *also* 2 Cor. 9. 6–10	Ezek. 9. 1–7; 10. 18–22 Ps. 113 Matt. 18. 15–20	Ps. 34 1 Sam. ch. 16 Luke 23. 44–56a	Ps. 119. 33–56 Jer. 33. 1–13 Jas. ch. 3
11 Thursday	**Clare of Assisi, Founder of the Minoresses (Poor Clares), 1253** *John Henry Newman, Priest, Tractarian, 1890*			
Gw	Com. Religious *or* *esp.* Song of Sol. 8. 6–7	Ezek. 12. 1–12 Ps. 78. 58–64 Matt. 18.21 – 19.1	Ps. 37† 1 Sam. 17. 1–30 Luke 23.56b – 24.12	Ps. 39; *40* Jer. 33. 14–end Jas. 4. 1–12
12 Friday				
G		Ezek. 16. 1–15, 60–end Ps. 118. 14–18 *or Canticle*: Song of Deliverance Matt. 19. 3–12	Ps. 31 1 Sam. 17. 31–54 Luke 24. 13–35	Ps. 35 Jer. ch. 35 Jas. 4.13 – 5.6
13 Saturday	**Jeremy Taylor, Bishop of Down and Connor, Teacher, 1667** *Florence Nightingale, Nurse, Social Reformer, 1910; Octavia Hill, Social Reformer, 1912*			
Gw	Com. Teacher *or* *also* Titus 2. 7–8, 11–14	Ezek. 18. 1–11a, 13b, 30, 32 Ps. 51. 1–3, 15–17 Matt. 19. 13–15	Ps. 41; *42*; 43 1 Sam. 17.55 – 18.16 Luke 24. 36–end	Ps. 45; *46* Jer. 36. 1–18 Jas. 5. 7–end **ct**

	Calendar and Holy Communion	Morning Prayer	Evening Prayer	NOTES
	THE TRANSFIGURATION OF OUR LORD			
w	Exod. 24. 12–end	(Ps. 27; 150)	(Ps. 72)	
	Ps. 84. 1–7	Ecclus. 48. 1–10	Exod. 34. 29–end	
	1 John 3. 1–3	or 1 Kings 19. 1–16	2 Cor. ch. 3	
	Mark 9. 2–7	2 Pet. 1. 16–19		
	THE EIGHTH SUNDAY AFTER TRINITY			
G	Jer. 23. 16–24	Ps. 115	Ps. 108; [116]	
	Ps. 31. 1–6	Song of Sol. 8. 5–7	Isa. 11.10 – 12.end	
	Rom. 8. 12–17	or 1 Macc. 14. 4–15	2 Cor. 1. 1–22	
	Matt. 7. 15–21	2 Pet. 3. 8–13		
G		1 Sam. 14. 24–46	Jer. 31. 23–25, 27–37	
		Luke 23. 13–25	Jas. 2. 1–13	
G		1 Sam. 15. 1–23	Jer. 32. 1–15	
		Luke 23. 26–43	Jas. 2. 14–end	
	Laurence, Deacon at Rome, Martyr, 258			
Gr	Com. Martyr	1 Sam. ch. 16	Jer. 33. 1–13	
		Luke 23. 44–56a	Jas. ch. 3	
G		1 Sam. 17. 1–30	Jer. 33. 14–end	
		Luke 23.56b – 24.12	Jas. 4. 1–12	
G		1 Sam. 17. 31–54	Jer. ch. 35	
		Luke 24. 13–35	Jas. 4.13 – 5.6	
G		1 Sam. 17.55 – 18.16	Jer. 36. 1–18	
		Luke 24. 36–end	Jas. 5. 7–end	
			ct	

		Sunday Principal Service Weekday Eucharist	Third Service Morning Prayer	Second Service Evening Prayer
14 Sunday	**THE NINTH SUNDAY AFTER TRINITY (Proper 15)**			
G		*Track 1* Isa. 5. 1–7 Ps. 80. 1–2, 9–end (or 80. 9–end) Heb. 11.29 – 12.2 Luke 12. 49–56	Ps. 119. 33–48 Jonah ch. 1 *or* Ecclus. 3. 1–15 2 Pet. 3. 14–end	Ps. 119. 17–32 (or 119. 17–24) Isa. 28. 9–22 2 Cor. 8. 1–9 *Gospel*: Matt. 20. 1–16 *or First EP of The* *Blessed Virgin Mary* Ps. 72 Prov. 8. 22–31 John 19. 23–27 **W ct**
		Track 2 Jer. 23. 23–29 Ps. 82 Heb. 11.29 – 12.2 Luke 12. 49–56		
15 Monday	**THE BLESSED VIRGIN MARY***			
W **DEL 20**		Isa. 61. 10–end *or* Rev. 11.19 – 12.6, 10 Ps. 45. 10–end Gal. 4. 4–7 Luke 1. 46–55	*MP*: Ps. 98; 138; 147. 1–12 Isa. 7. 10–15 Luke 11. 27–28	*EP*: Ps. 132 Song of Sol. 2. 1–7 Acts 1. 6–14
	or, if The Blessed Virgin Mary is celebrated on 8 September:			
G		Ezek. 24. 15–24 Ps. 78. 1–8 Matt. 19. 16–22	Ps. 44 1 Sam. 19. 1–18 Acts 1. 1–14	Ps. *47*; 49 Jer. 36. 19–end Mark 1. 1–13
16 Tuesday				
G		Ezek. 28. 1–10 Ps. 107. 1–3, 40, 43 Matt. 19. 23–end	Ps. *48*; 52 1 Sam. 20. 1–17 Acts 1. 15–end	Ps. 50 Jer. ch. 37 Mark 1. 14–20
17 Wednesday				
G		Ezek. 34. 1–11 Ps. 23 Matt. 20. 1–16	Ps. 119. 57–80 1 Sam. 20. 18–end Acts 2. 1–21	Ps. *59*; 60; (67) Jer. 38. 1–13 Mark 1. 21–28
18 Thursday				
G		Ezek. 36. 23–28 Ps. 51. 7–12 Matt. 22. 1–14	Ps. 56; *57*; (63†) 1 Sam. 21.1 – 22.5 Acts 2. 22–36	Ps. 61; *62*; 64 Jer. 38. 14–end Mark 1. 29–end
19 Friday				
G		Ezek. 37. 1–14 Ps. 107. 1–8 Matt. 22. 34–40	Ps. *51*; 54 1 Sam. 22. 6–end Acts 2. 37–end	Ps. 38 Jer. ch. 39 Mark 2. 1–12
20 Saturday	**Bernard, Abbot of Clairvaux, Teacher, 1153** *William and Catherine Booth, Founders of the Salvation Army, 1912 and 1890*			
Gw	Com. Religious *esp.* Rev. 19. 5–9 *or*	Ezek. 43. 1–7 Ps. 85. 7–end Matt. 23. 1–12	Ps. 68 1 Sam. ch. 23 Acts 3. 1–10	Ps. 65; *66* Jer. ch. 40 Mark 2. 13–22 **ct**
21 Sunday	**THE TENTH SUNDAY AFTER TRINITY (Proper 16)**			
G		*Track 1* Jer. 1. 4–10 Ps. 71. 1–6 Heb. 12. 18–end Luke 13. 10–17	Ps. 119. 73–88 Jonah ch. 2 *or* Ecclus. 3. 17–29 Rev. ch. 1	Ps. 119. 49–72 (or 119. 49–56) Isa. 30. 8–21 2 Cor. ch. 9 *Gospel*: Matt. 21. 28–32
		Track 2 Isa. 58. 9b–end Ps. 103. 1–8 Heb. 12. 18–end Luke 13. 10–17		

*The Blessed Virgin Mary may be celebrated on 8 September instead of 15 August.

	Calendar and Holy Communion	Morning Prayer	Evening Prayer	NOTES
	THE NINTH SUNDAY AFTER TRINITY			
G	Num. 10.35 – 11.3 Ps. 95 1 Cor. 10. 1–13 Luke 16. 1–9 or Luke 15. 11–end	Ps. 119. 33–48 Jonah ch. 1 or Ecclus. 3. 1–15 2 Pet. 3. 14–end	Ps. 119. 17–32 (or 119. 17–24) Isa. 28. 9–22 2 Cor. 8. 1–9	
	To celebrate The Blessed Virgin Mary, see Common Worship provision.			
G		1 Sam. 19. 1–18 Acts 1. 1–14	Jer. 36. 19–end Mark 1. 1–13	
G		1 Sam. 20. 1–17 Acts 1. 15–end	Jer. ch. 37 Mark 1. 14–20	
G		1 Sam. 20. 18–end Acts 2. 1–21	Jer. 38. 1–13 Mark 1. 21–28	
G		1 Sam. 21.1 – 22.5 Acts 2. 22–36	Jer. 38. 14–end Mark 1. 29–end	
G		1 Sam. 22. 6–end Acts 2. 37–end	Jer. ch. 39 Mark 2. 1–12	
G		1 Sam. ch. 23 Acts 3. 1–10	Jer. ch. 40 Mark 2. 13–22	
			ct	
	THE TENTH SUNDAY AFTER TRINITY			
G	Jer. 7. 9–15 Ps. 17. 1–8 1 Cor. 12. 1–11 Luke 19. 41–47a	Ps. 119. 73–88 Jonah ch. 2 or Ecclus. 3. 17–29 Rev. ch. 1	Ps. 119. 49–72 (or 119. 49–56) Isa. 30. 8–21 2 Cor. ch. 9	

		Sunday Principal Service / Weekday Eucharist	Third Service / Morning Prayer	Second Service / Evening Prayer
22 Monday				
G **DEL 21**		2 Thess. 1. 1–5, 11–end Ps. 39. 1–9 Matt. 23. 13–22	Ps. 71 1 Sam. ch. 24 Acts 3. 11–end	Ps. *72*; 75 Jer. ch. 41 Mark 2.23 – 3.6
23 Tuesday				
G		2 Thess. 2. 1–3a, 14–end Ps. 98 Matt. 23. 23–26	Ps. 73 1 Sam. ch. 26 Acts 4. 1–12	Ps. 74 Jer. ch. 42 Mark 3. 7–19a *or First EP of Bartholomew* Ps. 97 Isa. 61. 1–9 2 Cor. 6. 1–10 **R ct**
24 Wednesday	**BARTHOLOMEW THE APOSTLE**			
R		Isa. 43. 8–13 *or* Acts 5. 12–16 Ps. 145. 1–7 Acts 5. 12–16 *or* 1 Cor. 4. 9–15 Luke 22. 24–30	*MP*: Ps. 86; 117 Gen. 28. 10–17 John 1. 43–end	*EP*: Ps. 91; 116 Ecclus. 39. 1–10 *or* Deut. 18. 15–19 Matt. 10. 1–22
25 Thursday				
G		1 Cor. 1. 1–9 Ps. 145. 1–7 Matt. 24. 42–end	Ps. 78. 1–39† 1 Sam. ch. 31 Acts 4.32 – 5.11	Ps. 78. 40–end† Jer. 44. 1–14 Mark 4. 1–20
26 Friday				
G		1 Cor. 1. 17–25 Ps. 33. 6–12 Matt. 25. 1–13	Ps. 55 2 Sam. ch. 1 Acts 5. 12–26	Ps. 69 Jer. 44. 15–end Mark 4. 21–34
27 Saturday	**Monica, Mother of Augustine of Hippo, 387**			
Gw		Com. Saint *or* 1 Cor. 1. 26–end *also* Ecclus. 26. 1–3, Ps. 33. 12–15, 20–end 13–16 Matt. 25. 14–30	Ps. *76*; 79 2 Sam. 2. 1–11 Acts 5. 27–end	Ps. *81*; 84 Jer. ch. 45 Mark 4. 35–end **ct**
28 Sunday	**THE ELEVENTH SUNDAY AFTER TRINITY (Proper 17)**			
G		*Track 1* *Track 2* Jer. 2. 4–13 Ecclus. 10. 12–18 Ps. 81. 1, 10–end *or* Prov. 25. 6–7 (*or* 81. 1–11) Ps. 112 Heb. 13. 1–8, 15–16 Heb. 13. 1–8, 15–16 Luke 14. 1, 7–14 Luke 14. 1, 7–14	Ps. 119. 161–end Jonah 3. 1–9 *or* Ecclus. 11. [7–17] 18–28 Rev. 3. 14–22	Ps. 119. 81–96 (*or* 119. 81–88) Isa. 33. 13–22 John 3. 22–36
29 Monday	**The Beheading of John the Baptist**			
Gr **DEL 22**		Jer. 1. 4–10 *or* 1 Cor. 2. 1–5 Ps. 11 Ps. 33. 12–21 Heb. 11.32 – 12.2 Luke 4. 16–30 Matt. 14. 1–12	Ps. *80*; 82 2 Sam. 3. 12–end Acts ch. 6	Ps. *85*; 86 Mic. 1. 1–9 Mark 5. 1–20
30 Tuesday	**John Bunyan, Spiritual Writer, 1688**			
Gw		Com. Teacher *or* 1 Cor. 2. 10b–end *also* Heb. 12. 1–2 Ps. 145. 10–17 Luke 21. 21, 34–36 Luke 4. 31–37	Ps. 87; *89. 1–18* 2 Sam. 5. 1–12 Acts 7. 1–16	Ps. 89. 19–end Mic. ch. 2 Mark 5. 21–34

	Calendar and Holy Communion	Morning Prayer	Evening Prayer	NOTES
G		1 Sam. ch. 24 Acts 3. 11–end	Jer. ch. 41 Mark 2.23 – 3.6	
G		1 Sam. ch. 26 Acts 4. 1–12	Jer. ch. 42 Mark 3. 7–19a *or First EP of Bartholomew* (Ps. 97) Isa. 61. 1–9 2 Cor. 6. 1–10 **R ct**	
	BARTHOLOMEW THE APOSTLE			
R	Gen. 28. 10–17 Ps. 15 Acts 5. 12–16 Luke 22. 24–30	(Ps. 86; 117) Isa. 43. 8–13 John 1. 43–end	(Ps. 91; 116) Ecclus. 39. 1–10 *or* Deut. 18. 15–19 Matt. 10. 1–22	
G		1 Sam. ch. 31 Acts 4.32 – 5.11	Jer. 44. 1–14 Mark 4. 1–20	
G		2 Sam. ch. 1 Acts 5. 12–26	Jer. 44. 15–end Mark 4. 21–34	
G		2 Sam. 2. 1–11 Acts 5. 27–end	Jer. ch. 45 Mark 4. 35–end **ct**	
	THE ELEVENTH SUNDAY AFTER TRINITY			
G	1 Kings 3. 5–15 Ps. 28 1 Cor. 15. 1–11 Luke 18. 9–14	Ps. 119. 161–end Jonah 3. 1–9 *or* Ecclus. 11. [7–17] 18–28 Rev. 3. 14–22	Ps. 119. 81–96 (*or* 119. 81–88) Isa. 33. 13–22 John 3. 22–36	
	The Beheading of John the Baptist			
Gr	2 Chron. 24. 17–21 Ps. 92. 11–end Heb. 11.32 – 12.2 Matt. 14. 1–12	2 Sam. 3. 12–end Acts ch. 6	Mic. 1. 1–9 Mark 5. 1–20	
G		2 Sam. 5. 1–12 Acts 7. 1–16	Mic. ch. 2 Mark 5. 21–34	

		Sunday Principal Service Weekday Eucharist	Third Service Morning Prayer	Second Service Evening Prayer

31 Wednesday **Aidan, Bishop of Lindisfarne, Missionary, 651**

Gw	Com. Missionary *or* *also* 1 Cor. 9. 16–19	1 Cor. 3. 1–9 Ps. 62 Luke 4. 38–end	Ps. 119. 105–128 2 Sam. 6. 1–19 Acts 7. 17–43	Ps. *91*; 93 Mic. ch. 3 Mark 5. 35–end

September 2022

1 Thursday   *Giles of Provence, Hermit, c. 710*

G		1 Cor. 3. 18–end Ps. 24. 1–6 Luke 5. 1–11	Ps. 90; *92* 2 Sam. 7. 1–17 Acts 7. 44–53	Ps. 94 Mic. 4.1 – 5.1 Mark 6. 1–13

2 Friday   *The Martyrs of Papua New Guinea, 1901 and 1942*

G		1 Cor. 4. 1–5 Ps. 37. 3–8 Luke 5. 33–end	Ps. *88*; (95) 2 Sam. 7. 18–end Acts 7.54 – 8.3	Ps. 102 Mic. 5. 2–end Mark 6. 14–29

3 Saturday   **Gregory the Great, Bishop of Rome, Teacher, 604**

Gw	Com. Teacher *or* *also* 1 Thess. 2. 3–8	1 Cor. 4. 6–15 Ps. 145. 18–end Luke 6. 1–5	Ps. 96; *97*; 100 2 Sam. ch. 9 Acts 8. 4–25	Ps. 104 Mic. ch. 6 Mark 6. 30–44 ct

4 **Sunday**   **THE TWELFTH SUNDAY AFTER TRINITY (Proper 18)**

G	*Track 1* Jer. 18. 1–11 Ps. 139. 1–5, 12–18 (or 139. 1–7) Philem. 1–21 Luke 14. 25–33	*Track 2* Deut. 30. 15–end Ps. 1 Philem. 1–21 Luke 14. 25–33	Ps. 122; 123 Jonah 3.10 – 4.end *or* Ecclus. 27.30 – 28.9 Rev. 8. 1–5	Ps. [120]; 121 Isa. 43.14 – 44.5 John 5. 30–end

5 Monday

G **DEL 23**		1 Cor. 5. 1–8 Ps. 5. 5–9a Luke 6. 6–11	Ps. *98*; 99; 101 2 Sam. ch. 11 Acts 8. 26–end	Ps. *105*† (*or* 103) Mic. 7. 1–7 Mark 6. 45–end

6 Tuesday   *Allen Gardiner, Founder of the South American Mission Society, 1851*

G		1 Cor. 6. 1–11 Ps. 149. 1–5 Luke 6. 12–19	Ps. *106*† (*or* 103) 2 Sam. 12. 1–25 Acts 9. 1–19a	Ps. 107† Mic. 7. 8–end Mark 7. 1–13

7 Wednesday

G		1 Cor. 7. 25–31 Ps. 45. 11–end Luke 6. 20–26	Ps. 110; *111*; 112 2 Sam. 15. 1–12 Acts 9. 19b–31	Ps. 119. 129–152 Hab. 1. 1–11 Mark 7. 14–23

8 Thursday   **The Birth of the Blessed Virgin Mary***

Gw	Com. BVM *or*	1 Cor. 8. 1–7, 11–end Ps. 139. 1–9 Luke 6. 27–38	Ps. 113; *115* 2 Sam. 15. 13–end Acts 9. 32–end	Ps. 114; *116*; 117 Hab. 1.12 – 2.5 Mark 7. 24–30

9 Friday   *Charles Fuge Lowder, Priest, 1880*

G		1 Cor. 9. 16–19, 22–end Ps. 84. 1–6 Luke 6. 39–42	Ps. 139 2 Sam. 16. 1–14 Acts 10. 1–16	Ps. *130*; 131; 137 Hab. 2. 6–end Mark 7. 31–end

*The Blessed Virgin Mary may be celebrated on 8 September instead of 15 August.

	Calendar and Holy Communion	Morning Prayer	Evening Prayer	NOTES
G		2 Sam. 6. 1–19 Acts 7. 17–43	Mic. ch. 3 Mark 5. 35–end	

	Giles of Provence, Hermit, c. 710			
Gw	Com. Abbot	2 Sam. 7. 1–17 Acts 7. 44–53	Mic. 4.1 – 5.1 Mark 6. 1–13	
G		2 Sam. 7. 18–end Acts 7.54 – 8.3	Mic. 5. 2–end Mark 6. 14–29	
G		2 Sam. ch. 9 Acts 8. 4–25	Mic. ch. 6 Mark 6. 30–44	
			ct	

	THE TWELFTH SUNDAY AFTER TRINITY			
G	Exod. 34. 29–end Ps. 34. 1–10 2 Cor. 3. 4–9 Mark 7. 31–37	Ps. 123; 133 Jonah 3.10 – 4.end or Ecclus. 27.30 – 28.9 Rev. 8. 1–5	Ps. [120]; 121 Isa. 43.14 – 44.5 John 5. 30–end	
G		2 Sam. ch. 11 Acts 8. 26–end	Mic. 7. 1–7 Mark 6. 45–end	
G		2 Sam. 12. 1–25 Acts 9. 1–19a	Mic. 7. 8–end Mark 7. 1–13	

	Evurtius, Bishop of Orleans, 4th century			
Gw	Com. Bishop	2 Sam. 15. 1–12 Acts 9. 19b–31	Hab. 1. 1–11 Mark 7. 14–23	

	The Nativity of the Blessed Virgin Mary			
Gw	Gen. 3. 9–15 Ps. 45. 11–18 Rom. 5. 12–17 Luke 11. 27–28	2 Sam. 15. 13–end Acts 9. 32–end	Hab. 1.12 – 2.5 Mark 7. 24–30	
G		2 Sam. 16. 1–14 Acts 10. 1–16	Hab. 2. 6–end Mark 7. 31–end	

	Sunday Principal Service / Weekday Eucharist	Third Service / Morning Prayer	Second Service / Evening Prayer
10 Saturday			
G	1 Cor. 10. 14–22 Ps. 116. 10–end Luke 6. 43–end	Ps. 120; *121*; 122 2 Sam. 17. 1–23 Acts 10. 17–33	Ps. 118 Hab. 3. 2–19a Mark 8. 1–10 **ct**
11 Sunday	**THE THIRTEENTH SUNDAY AFTER TRINITY (Proper 19)**		
G	*Track 1* Jer. 4. 11–12, 22–28 Ps. 14 1 Tim. 1. 12–17 Luke 15. 1–10 *Track 2* Exod. 32. 7–14 Ps. 51. 1–11 1 Tim. 1. 12–17 Luke 15. 1–10	Ps. 126; 127 Isa. 44.24 – 45.8 Rev. 12. 1–12	Ps. 124; 125 Isa. ch. 60 John 6. 51–69
12 Monday			
G **DEL 24**	1 Cor. 11. 17–26, 33 Ps. 40. 7–11 Luke 7. 1–10	Ps. 123; 124; 125; *126* 2 Sam. 18. 1–18 Acts 10. 34–end	Ps. *127*; 128; 129 Hag. 1. 1–11 Mark 8. 11–21
13 Tuesday	John Chrysostom, Bishop of Constantinople, Teacher, 407		
Gw	Com. Teacher *or* 1 Cor. 12. 12–14, 27–end *esp.* Matt. 5. 13–19 Ps. 100 *also* Jer. 1. 4–10 Luke 7. 11–17	Ps. *132*; 133 2 Sam. 18.19 – 19.8a Acts 11. 1–18	Ps. (134); *135* Hag. 1.12 – 2.9 Mark 8. 22–26 *or First EP of Holy Cross Day* Ps. 66 Isa, 52.13 – 53.end Eph. 2. 11–end **R ct**
14 Wednesday	**HOLY CROSS DAY**		
R	Num. 21. 4–9 Ps. 22. 23–28 Phil. 2. 6–11 John 3. 13–17	*MP*: Ps. 2; 8; 146 Gen. 3. 1–15 John 12. 27–36a	*EP*: Ps. 110; 150 Isa. 63. 1–16 1 Cor. 1. 18–25
15 Thursday	Cyprian, Bishop of Carthage, Martyr, 258		
Gr	Com. Martyr *or* 1 Cor. 15. 1–11 *esp.* 1 Pet. 4. 12–end Ps. 118. 1–2, 17–20 *also* Matt. 18. 18–22 Luke 7. 36–end	Ps. *143*; 146 2 Sam. 19. 24–end Acts 12. 1–17	Ps. *138*; 140; 141 Zech. 1. 1–17 Mark 9. 2–13
16 Friday	Ninian, Bishop of Galloway, Apostle of the Picts, *c.* 432 *Edward Bouverie Pusey, Priest, Tractarian, 1882*		
Gw	Com. Missionary *or* 1 Cor. 15. 12–20 *esp.* Acts 13. 46–49 Ps. 17. 1–8 Mark 16. 15–end Luke 8. 1–3	Ps. 142; *144* 2 Sam. 23. 1–7 Acts 12. 18–end	Ps. 145 Zech. 1.18 – 2.end Mark 9. 14–29
17 Saturday	Hildegard, Abbess of Bingen, Visionary, 1179		
Gw	Com. Religious *or* 1 Cor. 15. 35–37, 42–49 *also* 1 Cor. 2. 9–13 Ps. 30. 1–5 Luke 10. 21–24 Luke 8. 4–15	Ps. 147 2 Sam. ch. 24 Acts 13. 1–12	Ps. *148*; 149; 150 Zech. ch. 3 Mark 9. 30–37 **ct**
18 Sunday	**THE FOURTEENTH SUNDAY AFTER TRINITY (Proper 20)**		
G	*Track 1* Jer. 8.18 – 9.1 Ps. 79. 1–9 1 Tim. 2. 1–7 Luke 16. 1–13 *Track 2* Amos 8. 4–7 Ps. 113 1 Tim. 2. 1–7 Luke 16. 1–13	Ps. 130; 131 Isa. 45. 9–22 Rev. 14. 1–5	Ps. [128]; 129 Ezra ch. 1 John 7. 14–36

	Calendar and Holy Communion	Morning Prayer	Evening Prayer	NOTES
G		2 Sam. 17. 1–23 Acts 10. 17–33	Hab. 3. 2–19a Mark 8. 1–10	
			ct	

THE THIRTEENTH SUNDAY AFTER TRINITY

G	Lev. 19. 13–18 Ps. 74. 20–end Gal. 3. 16–22 or Heb. 13. 1–6 Luke 10. 23b–37	Ps. 126; 127 Isa. 44.24 – 45.8 Rev. 12. 1–12	Ps. 124; 125 Isa. ch. 60 John 6. 51–69	
G		2 Sam. 18. 1–18 Acts 10. 34–end	Hag. 1. 1–11 Mark 8. 11–21	
G		2 Sam. 18.19 – 19.8a Acts 11. 1–18	Hag. 1.12 – 2.9 Mark 8. 22–26	

HOLY CROSS DAY
To celebrate Holy Cross as a festival, see *Common Worship* provision.

Gr	Num. 21. 4–9 Ps. 67 1 Cor. 1. 17–25 John 12. 27–33	2 Sam. 19. 8b–23 Acts 11. 19–end	Hag. 2. 10–end Mark 8.27 – 9.1	
G		2 Sam. 19. 24–end Acts 12. 1–17	Zech. 1. 1–17 Mark 9. 2–13	
G		2 Sam. 23. 1–7 Acts 12. 18–end	Zech. 1.18 – 2.end Mark 9. 14–29	

Lambert, Bishop of Maastricht, Martyr, 709

Gr	Com. Martyr	2 Sam. ch. 24 Acts 13. 1–12	Zech. ch. 3 Mark 9. 30–37	
			ct	

THE FOURTEENTH SUNDAY AFTER TRINITY

G	2 Kings 5. 9–16 Ps. 118. 1–9 Gal. 5. 16–24 Luke 17. 11–19	Ps. 130; 131 Isa. 45. 9–22 Rev. 14. 1–5	Ps. [128]; 129 Ezra ch. 1 John 7. 14–36	

		Sunday Principal Service Weekday Eucharist	Third Service Morning Prayer	Second Service Evening Prayer
19 Monday	*Theodore of Tarsus, Archbishop of Canterbury, 690*			
G **DEL 25**		Prov. 3. 27–34 Ps. 15 Luke 8. 16–18	Ps. *1*; 2; 3 1 Kings 1. 5–31 Acts 13. 13–43	Ps. *4*; 7 Zech. ch. 4 Mark 9. 38–end
20 Tuesday	*John Coleridge Patteson, first Bishop of Melanesia, and his Companions, Martyrs, 1871*			
Gr	Com. Martyr *or* *esp.* 2 Chron. 24. 17–21 *also* Acts 7. 55–end	Prov. 21. 1–6, 10–13 Ps. 119. 1–8 Luke 8. 19–21	Ps. *5*; 6; (8) 1 Kings 1.32 – 2.4, 10–12 Acts 13.44 – 14.7	Ps. *9*; 10† Zech. 6. 9–end Mark 10. 1–16 *or First EP of Matthew* Ps. 34 Isa. 33. 13–17 Matt. 6. 19–end **R** ct
21 Wednesday	**MATTHEW, APOSTLE AND EVANGELIST**			
R		Prov. 3. 13–18 Ps. 119. 65–72 2 Cor. 4. 1–6 Matt. 9. 9–13	*MP:* Ps. 49; 117 1 Kings 19. 15–end 2 Tim. 3. 14–end	*EP:* Ps. 119. 33–40, 89–96 Eccles. 5. 4–12 Matt. 19. 16–end
22 Thursday				
G		Eccles. 1. 2–11 Ps. 90. 1–6 Luke 9. 7–9	Ps. 14; *15*; 16 1 Kings 4.29 – 5.12 Acts 15. 1–21	Ps. 18† Zech. 8. 1–8 Mark 10. 32–34
23 Friday				
G		Eccles. 3. 1–11 Ps. 144. 1–4 Luke 9. 18–22	Ps. 17; *19* 1 Kings 6. 1, 11–28 Acts 15. 22–35	Ps. 22 Zech. 8. 9–end Mark 10. 35–45
24 Saturday				
G		Eccles. 11.9 – 12.8 Ps. 90. 1–2, 12–end Luke 9. 43b–45	Ps. 20; 21; *23* 1 Kings 8. 1–30 Acts 15.36 – 16.5	Ps. *24*; 25 Zech. 9. 1–12 Mark 10. 46–end ct
25 Sunday	**THE FIFTEENTH SUNDAY AFTER TRINITY (Proper 21)**			
G	*Track 1* Jer. 32. 1–3a, 6–15 Ps. 91. 1–6, 14–end (*or* 91. 11–end) 1 Tim. 6. 6–19 Luke 16. 19–end	*Track 2* Amos. 6. 1a, 4–7 Ps. 146 1 Tim. 6. 6–19 Luke 16. 19–end	Ps. 132 Isa. 48. 12–end Luke 11. 37–end	Ps. 134; 135 (*or* Ps. 135. 1–14) Neh. ch. 2 John 8. 31–38, 48–end
26 Monday	*Wilson Carlile, Founder of the Church Army, 1942*			
G **DEL 26**		Job 1. 6–end Ps. 17. 1–11 Luke 9. 46–50	Ps. 27; *30* 1 Kings 8. 31–62 Acts 16. 6–24	Ps. 26; *28*; 29 Zech. ch. 10 Mark 11. 1–11
27 Tuesday	*Vincent de Paul, Founder of the Congregation of the Mission (Lazarists), 1660*			
Gw	Com. Religious *or* *also* 1 Cor. 1. 25–end Matt. 25. 34–40	Job 3. 1–3, 11–17, 20–23 Ps. 88. 14–19 Luke 9. 51–56	Ps. 32; *36* 1 Kings 8.63 – 9.9 Acts 16. 25–end	Ps. 33 Zech. 11. 4–end Mark 11. 12–26

	Calendar and Holy Communion	Morning Prayer	Evening Prayer	NOTES
G		1 Kings 1. 5–31 Acts 13. 13–43	Zech. ch. 4 Mark 9. 38–end	
G		1 Kings 1.32 – 2.4, 10–12 Acts 13.44 – 14.7	Zech. 6. 9–end Mark 10. 1–16 or First EP of Matthew (Ps. 34) Prov. 3. 3–18 Matt. 6. 19–end	
			R ct	
	MATTHEW, APOSTLE AND EVANGELIST Ember Day			
R	Isa. 33. 13–17 Ps. 119. 65–72 2 Cor. 4. 1–6 Matt. 9. 9–13	(Ps. 49; 117) 1 Kings 19. 15–end 2 Tim. 3. 14–end	(Ps. 119. 33–40, 89–96) Eccles. 5. 4–12 Matt. 19. 16–end	
G		1 Kings 4.29 – 5.12 Acts 15. 1–21	Zech. 8. 1–8 Mark 10. 32–34	
	Ember Day			
G	Ember CEG	1 Kings 6. 1, 11–28 Acts 15. 22–35	Zech. 8. 9–end Mark 10. 35–45	
	Ember Day			
G	Ember CEG	1 Kings 8. 1–30 Acts 15.36 – 16.5	Zech. 9. 1–12 Mark 10. 46–end	
			ct	
	THE FIFTEENTH SUNDAY AFTER TRINITY			
G	Josh. 24. 14–25 Ps. 92. 1–6 Gal. 6. 11–end Matt. 6. 24–end	Ps. 132 Isa. 48. 12–end Luke 11. 37–end	Ps. 134; 135 (or Ps. 135. 1–14) Neh. ch. 2 John 8. 31–38, 48–end	
	Cyprian, Bishop of Carthage, Martyr, 258			
Gr	Com. Martyr	1 Kings 8. 31–62 Acts 16. 6–24	Zech. ch. 10 Mark 11. 1–11	
G		1 Kings 8.63 – 9.9 Acts 16. 25–end	Zech. 11. 4–end Mark 11. 12–26	

	Sunday Principal Service Weekday Eucharist	Third Service Morning Prayer	Second Service Evening Prayer

28 Wednesday   Ember Day*

G *or* **R**	Job 9. 1–12, 14–16 Ps. 88. 1–6, 11 Luke 9. 57–end	Ps. 34 1 Kings 10. 1–25 Acts 17. 1–15	Ps. 119. 33–56 Zech. 12. 1–10 Mark 11. 27–end *or First EP of Michael and All Angels* Ps. 91 2 Kings 6. 8–17 Matt. 18. 1–6, 10 **W ct**

29 Thursday   **MICHAEL AND ALL ANGELS**

W	Gen. 28. 10–17 *or* Rev. 12. 7–12 Ps. 103. 19–end Rev. 12. 7–12 *or* Heb. 1. 5–end John 1. 47–end	*MP*: Ps. 34; 150 Tobit 12. 6–end *or* Dan. 12. 1–4 Acts 12. 1–11	*EP*: Ps. 138; 148 Dan. 10. 4–end Rev. ch. 5

30 Friday   Ember Day*
Jerome, Translator of the Scriptures, Teacher, 420

G *or* **R**	Job 38. 1, 12–21; 40. 3–5 Ps. 139. 6–11 Luke 10. 13–16	Ps. 31 1 Kings 11. 26–end Acts 18. 1–21	Ps. 35 Zech. 14. 1–11 Mark 12. 13–17

October 2022

1 Saturday   Ember Day*
Remigius, Bishop of Rheims, Apostle of the Franks, 533; Anthony Ashley Cooper, Earl of Shaftesbury,
Social Reformer, 1885

G *or* **R**	Job 42. 1–3, 6, 12–end Ps. 119. 169–end Luke 10. 17–24	Ps. 41; *42*; 43 1 Kings 12. 1–24 Acts 18.22 – 19.7	Ps. 45; *46* Zech. 14. 12–end Mark 12. 18–27 **ct** *or First EP of Dedication Festival* Ps. 24 2 Chron. 7. 11–16 John 4. 19–29 𝖂 **ct**

2 Sunday   **THE SIXTEENTH SUNDAY AFTER TRINITY (Proper 22)**

G	*Track 1* Lam. 1. 1–6 *Canticle*: Lam. 3. 19–26 *or* Ps. 137 (*or* 137. 1–6) 2 Tim. 1. 1–14 Luke 17. 5–10	*Track 2* Hab. 1. 1–4; 2. 1–4 Ps. 37. 1–9 2 Tim. 1. 1–14 Luke 17. 5–10	Ps. 141 Isa. 49. 13–23 Luke 12. 1–12	Ps. 142 Neh. 5. 1–13 John ch. 9
	or, if observed as Dedication Festival:			
𝖂		1 Chron. 29. 6–19 Ps. 122 Eph. 2. 19–end John 2. 13–22	*MP*: Ps. 48; 150 Hag. 2. 6–9 Heb. 10. 19–25	*EP*: Ps. 132 Jer. 7. 1–11 Luke 19. 1–10

*For Ember Day provision, see p. 11.

	Calendar and Holy Communion	Morning Prayer	Evening Prayer	NOTES
G		1 Kings 10. 1–25 Acts 17. 1–15	Zech. 12. 1–10 Mark 11. 27–end *or First EP of Michael* *and All Angels* (Ps. 91) 2 Kings 6. 8–17 John 1. 47–51	
			W ct	

MICHAEL AND ALL ANGELS

W	Dan. 10. 10–19a Ps. 103. 17–22 Rev. 12. 7–12 Matt. 18. 1–10	(Ps. 34; 150) Tobit 12. 6–end *or* Dan. 12. 1–4 Acts 12. 1–11	(Ps. 138; 148) Gen. 28. 10–17 Rev. ch. 5	

Jerome, Translator of the Scriptures, Teacher, 420

Gw	Com. Doctor	1 Kings 11. 26–end Acts 18. 1–21	Zech. 14. 1–11 Mark 12. 13–17	

Remigius, Bishop of Rheims, Apostle of the Franks, 533

Gw	Com. Bishop	1 Kings 12. 1–24 Acts 18.22 – 19.7	Zech. 14. 12–end Mark 12. 18–27 **ct** *or First EP of* *Dedication Festival* Ps. 24 2 Chron. 7. 11–16 John 4. 19–29	
			𝖂 ct	

THE SIXTEENTH SUNDAY AFTER TRINITY

G	1 Kings 17. 17–end Ps. 102. 12–17 Eph. 3. 13–end Luke 7. 11–17	Ps. 141 Isa. 49. 13–23 Luke 12. 1–12	Ps. 142 Neh. 5. 1–13 John ch. 9	
	or, if observed as Dedication Festival:			
𝖂	2 Chron. 7. 11–16 Ps. 122 1 Cor. 3. 9–17 *or* 1 Pet. 2. 1–5 Matt. 21. 12–16 *or* John 10. 22–29	Ps. 48; 150 Hag. 2. 6–9 Heb. 10. 19–25	Ps. 132 Jer. 7. 1–11 Luke 19. 1–10	

		Sunday Principal Service Weekday Eucharist	Third Service Morning Prayer	Second Service Evening Prayer
3 Monday	*George Bell, Bishop of Chichester, Ecumenist, Peacemaker, 1958*			
G **DEL 27**		Gal. 1. 6–12 Ps. 111. 1–6 Luke 10. 25–37	Ps. 44 1 Kings 12.25 – 13.10 Acts 19. 8–20	Ps. **47**; 49 Ecclus. 1. 1–10 *or* Ezek. 1. 1–14 Mark 12. 28–34
4 Tuesday	**Francis of Assisi, Friar, Founder of the Friars Minor, 1226**			
Gw	Com. Religious *or* *also* Gal. 6. 14–end Luke 12. 22–34	Gal. 1. 13–end Ps. 139. 1–9 Luke 10. 38–end	Ps. **48**; 52 1 Kings 13. 11–end Acts 19. 21–end	Ps. 50 Ecclus. 1. 11–end *or* Ezek. 1.15 – 2.2 Mark 12. 35–end
5 Wednesday				
G		Gal. 2. 1–2, 7–14 Ps. 117 Luke 11. 1–4	Ps. 119. 57–80 1 Kings ch. 17 Acts 20. 1–16	Ps. **59**; 60; (67) Ecclus. ch. 2 *or* Ezek. 2.3 – 3.11 Mark 13. 1–13
6 Thursday	**William Tyndale, Translator of the Scriptures, Reformation Martyr, 1536**			
Gr	Com. Martyr *or* *also* Prov. 8. 4–11 2 Tim. 3. 12–end	Gal. 3. 1–5 *Canticle*: Benedictus Luke 11. 5–13	Ps. 56; **57**; (63†) 1 Kings 18. 1–20 Acts 20. 17–end	Ps. 61; **62**; 64 Ecclus. 3. 17–29 *or* Ezek. 3. 12–end Mark 13. 14–23
7 Friday				
G		Gal. 3. 7–14 Ps. 111. 4–end Luke 11. 15–26	Ps. **51**; 54 1 Kings 18. 21–end Acts 21. 1–16	Ps. 38 Ecclus. 4. 11–28 *or* Ezek. ch. 8 Mark 13. 24–31
8 Saturday				
G		Gal. 3. 22–end Ps. 105. 1–7 Luke 11. 27–28	Ps. 68 1 Kings ch. 19 Acts 21. 17–36	Ps. 65; **66** Ecclus. 4.29 – 6.1 *or* Ezek. ch. 9 Mark 13. 32–end **ct**
9 Sunday	**THE SEVENTEENTH SUNDAY AFTER TRINITY (Proper 23)**			
G	*Track 1* Jer. 29. 1, 4–7 Ps. 66. 1–11 2 Tim. 2. 8–15 Luke 17. 11–19	*Track 2* 2 Kings 5. 1–3, 7–15c Ps. 111 2 Tim. 2. 8–15 Luke 17. 11–19	Ps. 143 Isa. 50. 4–10 Luke 13. 22–30	Ps. 144 Neh. 6. 1–16 John 15. 12–end
10 Monday	**Paulinus, Bishop of York, Missionary, 644** *Thomas Traherne, Poet, Spiritual Writer, 1674*			
Gw **DEL 28**	Com. Missionary *or* *esp.* Matt. 28. 16–end	Gal. 4. 21–24, 26–27, 31; 5. 1 Ps. 113 Luke 11. 29–32	Ps. 71 1 Kings ch. 21 Acts 21.37 – 22.21	Ps. **72**; 75 Ecclus. 6. 14–end *or* Ezek. 10. 1–19 Mark 14. 1–11
11 Tuesday	*Ethelburga, Abbess of Barking, 675; James the Deacon, Companion of Paulinus, 7th century*			
G		Gal. 5. 1–6 Ps. 119. 41–48 Luke 11. 37–41	Ps. 73 1 Kings 22. 1–28 Acts 22.22 – 23.11	Ps. 74 Ecclus. 7. 27–end *or* Ezek. 11. 14–end Mark 14. 12–25

	Calendar and Holy Communion	Morning Prayer	Evening Prayer	NOTES
G		1 Kings 12.25 – 13.10 Acts 19. 8–20	Ecclus. 1. 1–10 or Ezek. 1. 1–14 Mark 12. 28–34	
G		1 Kings 13. 11–end Acts 19. 21–end	Ecclus. 1. 11–end or Ezek. 1.15 – 2.2 Mark 12. 35–end	
G		1 Kings ch. 17 Acts 20. 1–16	Ecclus. ch. 2 or Ezek. 2.3 – 3.11 Mark 13. 1–13	
	Faith of Aquitaine, Martyr, c. 304			
Gr	Com. Virgin Martyr	1 Kings 18. 1–20 Acts 20. 17–end	Ecclus. 3. 17–29 or Ezek. 3. 12–end Mark 13. 14–23	
G		1 Kings 18. 21–end Acts 21. 1–16	Ecclus. 4. 11–28 or Ezek. ch. 8 Mark 13. 24–31	
G		1 Kings ch. 19 Acts 21. 17–36	Ecclus. 4.29 – 6.1 or Ezek. ch. 9 Mark 13. 32–end	
			ct	
	THE SEVENTEENTH SUNDAY AFTER TRINITY			
G	Prov. 25. 6–14 Ps. 33. 6–12 Eph. 4. 1–6 Luke 14. 1–11	Ps. 143 Isa. 50. 4–10 Luke 13. 22–30	Ps. 144 Neh. 6. 1–16 John 15. 12–end	
G		1 Kings ch. 21 Acts 21.37 – 22.21	Ecclus. 6. 14–end or Ezek. 10. 1–19 Mark 14. 1–11	
G		1 Kings 22. 1–28 Acts 22.22 – 23.11	Ecclus. 7. 27–end or Ezek. 11. 14–end Mark 14. 12–25	

	Sunday Principal Service Weekday Eucharist	Third Service Morning Prayer	Second Service Evening Prayer
12 Wednesday	**Wilfrid of Ripon, Bishop, Missionary, 709** *Elizabeth Fry, Prison Reformer, 1845; Edith Cavell, Nurse, 1915*		
Gw	Com. Missionary *or* Gal. 5. 18–end *esp.* Luke 5. 1–11 Ps. 1 *also* 1 Cor. 1. 18–25 Luke 11. 42–46	Ps. 77 1 Kings 22. 29–45 Acts 23. 12–end	Ps. 119. 81–104 Ecclus. 10. 6–8, 12–24 *or* Ezek. 12. 1–16 Mark 14. 26–42
13 Thursday	**Edward the Confessor, King of England, 1066**		
Gw	Com. Saint *or* Eph. 1. 1–10 *also* 2 Sam. 23. 1–5 Ps. 98. 1–4 1 John 4. 13–16 Luke 11. 47–end	Ps. 78. 1–39† 2 Kings 1. 2–17 Acts 24. 1–23	Ps. 78. 40–end† Ecclus. 11. 7–28 *or* Ezek. 12. 17–end Mark 14. 43–52
14 Friday			
G	Eph. 1. 11–14 Ps. 33. 1–6, 12 Luke 12. 1–7	Ps. 55 2 Kings 2. 1–18 Acts 24.24 – 25.12	Ps. 69 Ecclus. 14.20 – 15.10 *or* Ezek. 13. 1–16 Mark 14. 53–65
15 Saturday	**Teresa of Avila, Teacher, 1582**		
Gw	Com. Teacher *or* Eph. 1. 15–end *also* Rom. 8. 22–27 Ps. 8 Luke 12. 8–12	Ps. *76*; 79 2 Kings 4. 1–37 Acts 25. 13–end	Ps. 81; *84* Ecclus. 15. 11–end *or* Ezek. 14. 1–11 Mark 14. 66–end **ct**
16 Sunday	**THE EIGHTEENTH SUNDAY AFTER TRINITY (Proper 24)**		
G	*Track 1* *Track 2* Jer. 31. 27–34 Gen. 32. 22–31 Ps. 119. 97–104 Ps. 121 2 Tim. 3.14 – 4.5 2 Tim. 3.14 – 4.5 Luke 18. 1–8 Luke 18. 1–8	Ps. 147 Isa. 54. 1–14 Luke 13. 31–end	Ps. [146]; 149 Neh. 8. 9–end John 16. 1–11
17 Monday	**Ignatius, Bishop of Antioch, Martyr, c. 107**		
Gr **DEL 29**	Com. Martyr *or* Eph. 2. 1–10 *also* Phil. 3. 7–12 Ps. 100 John 6. 52–58 Luke 12. 13–21	Ps. *80*; 82 2 Kings ch. 5 Acts 26. 1–23	Ps. *85*; 86 Ecclus. 16. 17–end *or* Ezek. 14. 12–end Mark 15. 1–15 *or First EP of Luke* Ps. 33 Hos. 6. 1–3 2 Tim. 3. 10–end **R ct**
18 Tuesday	**LUKE THE EVANGELIST**		
R	Isa. 35. 3–6 *or* Acts 16. 6–12a Ps. 147. 1–7 2 Tim. 4. 5–17 Luke 10. 1–9	*MP*: Ps. 145; 146 Isa. ch. 55 Luke 1. 1–4	*EP*: Ps. 103 Ecclus. 38. 1–14 *or* Isa. 61. 1–6 Col. 4. 7–end
19 Wednesday	**Henry Martyn, Translator of the Scriptures, Missionary in India and Persia, 1812**		
Gw	Com. Missionary *or* Eph. 3. 2–12 *esp.* Mark 16. 15–end Ps. 98 *also* Isa. 55. 6–11 Luke 12. 39–48	Ps. 119. 105–128 2 Kings 9. 1–16 Acts 27. 1–26	Ps. *91*; 93 Ecclus. 18. 1–14 *or* Ezek. 18. 21–32 Mark 15. 33–41

	Calendar and Holy Communion	Morning Prayer	Evening Prayer	NOTES
G		1 Kings 22. 29–45 Acts 23. 12–end	Ecclus. 10. 6–8, 12–24 *or* Ezek. 12. 1–16 Mark 14. 26–42	
	Edward the Confessor, King of England, 1066, translated 1163			
Gw	Com. Saint	2 Kings 1. 2–17 Acts 24. 1–23	Ecclus. 11. 7–28 *or* Ezek. 12. 17–end Mark 14. 43–52	
G		2 Kings 2. 1–18 Acts 24.24 – 25.12	Ecclus. 14.20 – 15.10 *or* Ezek. 13. 1–16 Mark 14. 53–65	
G		2 Kings 4. 1–37 Acts 25. 13–end	Ecclus. 15. 11–end *or* Ezek. 14. 1–11 Mark 14. 66–end **ct**	
	THE EIGHTEENTH SUNDAY AFTER TRINITY			
G	Deut. 6. 4–9 Ps. 122 1 Cor. 1. 4–8 Matt. 22. 34–end	Ps. 147 Isa. 54. 1–14 Luke 13. 31–end	Ps. [146]; 149 Neh. 8. 9–end John 16. 1–11	
	Etheldreda, Abbess of Ely, 679			
Gw	Com. Abbess	2 Kings ch. 5 Acts 26. 1–23	Ecclus. 16. 17–end *or* Ezek. 14. 12–end Mark 15. 1–15 *or First EP of Luke* (Ps. 33) Hos. 6. 1–3 2 Tim. 3. 10–end **R ct**	
	LUKE THE EVANGELIST			
R	Isa. 35. 3–6 Ps. 147. 1–6 2 Tim. 4. 5–15 Luke 10. 1–9 *or* Luke 7. 36–end	(Ps. 145; 146) Isa. ch. 55 Luke 1. 1–4	(Ps. 103) Ecclus. 38. 1–14 *or* Isa. 61. 1–6 Col. 4. 7–end	
G		2 Kings 9. 1–16 Acts 27. 1–26	Ecclus. 18. 1–14 *or* Ezek. 18. 21–32 Mark 15. 33–41	

	Sunday Principal Service / Weekday Eucharist	Third Service / Morning Prayer	Second Service / Evening Prayer
20 Thursday			
G	Eph. 3. 14–end Ps. 33. 1–6 Luke 12. 49–53	Ps. 90; *92* 2 Kings 9. 17–end Acts 27. 27–end	Ps. 94 Ecclus. 19. 4–17 *or* Ezek. 20. 1–20 Mark 15. 42–end
21 Friday			
G	Eph. 4. 1–6 Ps. 24. 1–6 Luke 12. 54–end	Ps. *88*; (95) 2 Kings 12. 1–19 Acts 28. 1–16	Ps. 102 Ecclus. 19. 20–end *or* Ezek. 20. 21–38 Mark 16. 1–8
22 Saturday			
G	Eph. 4. 7–16 Ps. 122 Luke 13. 1–9	Ps. 96; *97*; 100 2 Kings 17. 1–23 Acts 28. 17–end	Ps. 104 Ecclus. 21. 1–17 *or* Ezek. 24. 15–end Mark 16. 9–end **ct**
23 Sunday	**THE LAST SUNDAY AFTER TRINITY (Proper 25)***		
G	*Track 1* Joel 2. 23–end Ps. 65 (*or* 65. 1–7) 2 Tim. 4. 6–8, 16–18 Luke 18. 9–14	*Track 2* Ecclus. 35. 12–17 *or* Jer. 14. 7–10, 19–end Ps. 84. 1–7 2 Tim. 4. 6–8, 16–18 Luke 18. 9–14 [Third Service: Ps. 119. 105–128 Isa. 59. 9–20 Luke 14. 1–14]	Ps. 119. 1–16 Eccles. chs 11 & 12 2 Tim. 2. 1–7 *Gospel:* Matt. 22. 34–end
	or, if being observed as Bible Sunday:		
G		Isa. 45. 22–end Ps. 119. 129–136 Rom. 15. 1–6 Luke 4. 16–24 [Third Service: Ps. 119. 105–128 1 Kings 22. 1–17 Rom. 15. 4–13 *or* Luke 14. 1–14]	Ps. 119. 1–16 Jer. 36. 9–end Rom. 10. 5–17 *Gospel:* Matt. 22. 34–40
24 Monday			
G **DEL 30**	Eph. 4.32 – 5.8 Ps. 1 Luke 13. 10–17	Ps. *98*; 99; 101 2 Kings 17. 24–end Phil. 1. 1–11	Ps. *105*† (*or* 103) Ecclus. 22. 6–22 *or* Ezek. 28. 1–19 John 13. 1–11
25 Tuesday	*Crispin and Crispinian, Martyrs at Rome, c. 287*		
G	Eph. 5. 21–end Ps. 128 Luke 13. 18–21	Ps. *106*† (*or* 103) 2 Kings 18. 1–12 Phil. 1. 12–end	Ps. 107† Ecclus. 22.27 – 23.15 *or* Ezek. 33. 1–20 John 13. 12–20
26 Wednesday	**Alfred the Great, King of the West Saxons, Scholar, 899** *Cedd, Abbot of Lastingham, Bishop of the East Saxons, 664***		
Gw	Com. Saint *or* *also* 2 Sam. 23. 1–5 John 18. 33–37 [or: Eph. 6. 1–9 Ps. 145. 10–20 Luke 13. 22–30]	Ps. 110; *111*; 112 2 Kings 18. 13–end Phil. 2. 1–13	Ps. 119. 129–152 Ecclus. 24. 1–22 *or* Ezek. 33. 21–end John 13. 21–30

*If the Dedication Festival is kept on this Sunday, use the provision given on 1 and 2 October.
**Chad may be celebrated with Cedd on 26 October instead of 2 March.

	Calendar and Holy Communion	Morning Prayer	Evening Prayer	NOTES
G		2 Kings 9. 17–end Acts 27. 27–end	Ecclus. 19. 4–17 or Ezek. 20. 1–20 Mark 15. 42–end	
G		2 Kings 12. 1–19 Acts 28. 1–16	Ecclus. 19. 20–end or Ezek. 20. 21–38 Mark 16. 1–8	
G		2 Kings 17. 1–23 Acts 28. 17–end	Ecclus. 21. 1–17 or Ezek. 24. 15–end Mark 16. 9–end	
			ct	

THE NINETEENTH SUNDAY AFTER TRINITY

	Calendar and Holy Communion	Morning Prayer	Evening Prayer	NOTES
G	Gen. 18. 23–32 Ps. 141. 1–9 Eph. 4. 17–end Matt. 9. 1–8	Ps. 119. 105–128 Isa. 59. 9–20 Luke 14. 12–24	Ps. 119. 1–16 Eccles. chs 11 & 12 2 Tim. 2. 1–7	
G		2 Kings 17. 24–end Phil. 1. 1–11	Ecclus. 22. 6–22 or Ezek. 28. 1–19 John 13. 1–11	

Crispin, Martyr at Rome, c. 287

	Calendar and Holy Communion	Morning Prayer	Evening Prayer	NOTES
Gr	Com. Martyr	2 Kings 18. 1–12 Phil. 1. 12–end	Ecclus. 22.27 – 23.15 or Ezek. 33. 1–20 John 13. 12–20	
G		2 Kings 18. 13–end Phil. 2. 1–13	Ecclus. 24. 1–22 or Ezek. 33. 21–end John 13. 21–30	

	Sunday Principal Service Weekday Eucharist	Third Service Morning Prayer	Second Service Evening Prayer
27 Thursday			
G	Eph. 6. 10–20 Ps. 144. 1–2, 9–11 Luke 13. 31–end	Ps. 113; **115** 2 Kings 19. 1–19 Phil. 2. 14–end	Ps. 114; **116**; 117 Ecclus. 24. 23–end or Ezek. 34. 1–16 John 13. 31–end or *First EP of Simon and Jude* Ps. 124; 125; 126 Deut. 32. 1–4 John 14. 15–26 **R** ct
28 Friday	**SIMON AND JUDE, APOSTLES**		
R	Isa. 28. 14–16 Ps. 119. 89–96 Eph. 2. 19–end John 15. 17–end	*MP*: Ps. 116; 117 Wisd. 5. 1–16 or Isa. 45. 18–end Luke 6. 12–16	*EP*: Ps. 119. 1–16 1 Macc. 2. 42–66 or Jer. 3. 11–18 Jude 1–4, 17–end
29 Saturday	**James Hannington, Bishop of Eastern Equatorial Africa, Martyr in Uganda, 1885**		
Gr	Com. Martyr or *esp.* Matt. 10. 28–39	Phil. 1. 18–26 Ps. 42. 1–7 Luke 14. 1, 7–11	Ps. 120; **121**; 122 2 Kings ch. 20 Phil. 4. 2–end	Ps. 118 Ecclus. 28. 14–end or Ezek. 36. 16–36 John 14. 15–end ct
30 Sunday	**THE FOURTH SUNDAY BEFORE ADVENT**		
R or G		Isa. 1. 10–18 Ps. 32. 1–8 2 Thess. ch. 1 Luke 19. 1–10	Ps. 87 Job ch. 26 Col. 1. 9–14	Ps. 145 (or 145. 1–9) Lam. 3. 22–33 John 11. [1–31] 32–44
	or ALL SAINTS' SUNDAY (see readings for 1 November throughout the day)			
𝖂				
31 Monday	*Martin Luther, Reformer, 1546*		
R or G* **DEL 31**		Phil. 2. 1–4 Ps. 131 Luke 14. 12–14	Ps. **2**; 146 *alt.* Ps. 123; 124; 125; **126** Dan. ch. 1 Rev. ch. 1	*First EP of All Saints* Ps. 1; 5 Ecclus. 44. 1–15 or Isa. 40. 27–end Rev. 19. 6–10 𝖂 ct *or, if All Saints is observed on 30 October:* Ps. **92**; 96; 97 *alt.* Ps. **127**; 128; 129 Isa. 1. 1–20 Matt. 1. 18–end

*R or G if All Saints is celebrated on 30 October.

	Calendar and Holy Communion	Morning Prayer	Evening Prayer	NOTES
G		2 Kings 19. 1–19 Phil. 2. 14–end	Ecclus. 24. 23–end *or* Ezek. 34. 1–16 John 13. 31–end *or First EP of Simon and Jude* (Ps. 124; 125; 126) Deut. 32. 1–4 John 14. 15–26	
			R ct	
	SIMON AND JUDE, APOSTLES			
R	Isa. 28. 9–16 Ps. 116. 11–end Jude 1–8 *or* Rev. 21. 9–14 John 15. 17–end	(Ps. 119. 89–96) Wisd. 5. 1–16 *or* Isa. 45. 18–end Luke 6. 12–16	(Ps. 119. 1–16) 1 Macc. 2. 42–66 *or* Jer. 3. 11–18 Eph. 2. 19–end	
G		2 Kings ch. 20 Phil. 4. 2–end	Ecclus. 28. 14–end *or* Ezek. 36. 16–36 John 14. 15–end	
			ct	
	THE TWENTIETH SUNDAY AFTER TRINITY			
G	Prov. 9. 1–6 Ps. 145. 15–end Eph. 5. 15–21 Matt. 22. 1–14	Ps. 87 Job ch. 26 Luke 19. 1–10	Ps. 145 (*or* 145. 1–9) Lam. 3. 22–33 John 11. [1–31] 32–44	
G		Dan. ch. 1 Rev. ch. 1	*First EP of All Saints* Ps. 1; 5 Ecclus. 44. 1–15 *or* Isa. 40. 27–end Rev. 19. 6–10	
			𝔚 ct	

		Sunday Principal Service Weekday Eucharist	Third Service Morning Prayer	Second Service Evening Prayer

November 2022

1 Tuesday — ALL SAINTS' DAY

℣		Dan. 7. 1–3, 15–18 Ps. 149 Eph. 1. 11–end Luke 6. 20–31	*MP*: Ps. 15; 84; 149 Isa. ch. 35 Luke 9. 18–27	*EP*: Ps. 148; 150 Isa. 65. 17–end Heb. 11.32 – 12.2

or, if the readings above are used on Sunday 30 October:

℣		Isa. 56. 3–8 *or* 2 Esd. 2. 42–end Ps. 33. 1–5 Heb. 12. 18–24 Matt. 5. 1–12	*MP*: Ps. 111; 112; 117 Wisd. 5. 1–16 *or* Jer. 31. 31–34 2 Cor. 4. 5–12	*EP*: Ps. 145 Isa. 66. 20–23 Col. 1. 9–14

or, if kept as a feria:

R *or* G		Phil. 2. 5–11 Ps. 22. 22–27 Luke 14. 15–24	Ps. *5*; 147. 1–12 *alt.* Ps. *132*; 133 Dan. 2. 1–24 Rev. 2. 1–11	Ps. 98; 99; *100* *alt.* Ps. (134); *135* Isa. 1. 21–end Matt. 2. 1–15

2 Wednesday — Commemoration of the Faithful Departed (All Souls' Day)

Rp *or* Gp	Lam. 3. 17–26, 31–33 *or* *or* Wisd. 3. 1–9 Ps. 23 *or* Ps. 27. 1–6, 16–end Rom. 5. 5–11 *or* 1 Pet. 1. 3–9 John 5. 19–25 *or* John 6. 37–40	Phil. 2. 12–18 Ps. 27. 1–5 Luke 14. 25–33	Ps. *9*; 147. 13–end *alt.* Ps. 119. 153–end Dan. 2. 25–end Rev. 2. 12–end	Ps. 111; *112*; 116 *alt.* Ps. 136 Isa. 2. 1–11 Matt. 2. 16–end

3 Thursday

Richard Hooker, Priest, Anglican Apologist, Teacher, 1600
Martin of Porres, Friar, 1639

Rw *or* Gw	Com. Teacher *or* *esp.* John 16. 12–15 *also* Ecclus. 44. 10–15	Phil. 3. 3–8a Ps. 105. 1–7 Luke 15. 1–10	Ps. 11; *15*; 148 *alt.* Ps. *143*; 146 Dan. 3. 1–18 Rev. 3. 1–13	Ps. 118 *alt.* Ps. *138*; 140; 141 Isa. 2. 12–end Matt. ch. 3

4 Friday

R *or* G		Phil. 3.17 – 4.1 Ps. 122 Luke 16. 1–8	Ps. *16*; 149 *alt.* Ps. 142; *144* Dan. 3. 19–end Rev. 3. 14–end	Ps. 137; 138; *143* *alt.* Ps. 145 Isa. 3. 1–15 Matt. 4. 1–11

5 Saturday

R *or* G		Phil. 4. 10–19 Ps. 112 Luke 16. 9–15	Ps. *18. 31–end*; 150 *alt.* Ps. 147 Dan. 4. 1–18 Rev. ch. 4	Ps. 145 *alt.* Ps. *148*; 149; 150 Isa. 4.2 – 5.7 Matt. 4. 12–22 ct

6 Sunday — THE THIRD SUNDAY BEFORE ADVENT

R *or* G		Job 19. 23–27a Ps. 17. 1–9 (*or* 17. 1–8) 2 Thess. 2. 1–5, 13–end Luke 20. 27–38	Ps. 20; 90 Isa. 2. 1–5 Jas. 3. 13–end	Ps. 40 1 Kings 3. 1–15 Rom. 8. 31–end *Gospel*: Matt. 22. 15–22

	Calendar and Holy Communion	Morning Prayer	Evening Prayer	NOTES

ALL SAINTS' DAY

ℳ	Isa. 66. 20–23 Ps. 33. 1–5 Rev. 7. 2–4 [5–8] 9–12 Matt. 5. 1–12	Ps. 15; 84; 149 Isa. ch. 35 Luke 9. 18–27	Ps. 148; 150 Isa. 65. 17–end Heb. 11.32 – 12.2	

To celebrate All Souls' Day, see *Common Worship* provision.

G		Dan. 2. 25–end Rev. 2. 12–end	Isa. 2. 1–11 Matt. 2. 16–end	
G		Dan. 3. 1–18 Rev. 3. 1–13	Isa. 2. 12–end Matt. ch. 3	
G		Dan. 3. 19–end Rev. 3. 14–end	Isa. 3. 1–15 Matt. 4. 1–11	
G		Dan. 4. 1–18 Rev. ch. 4	Isa. 4.2 – 5.7 Matt. 4. 12–22	

ct

THE TWENTY-FIRST SUNDAY AFTER TRINITY

G	Gen. 32. 24–29 Ps. 90. 1–12 Eph. 6. 10–20 John 4. 46b–end	Ps. 20; 90 Isa. 2. 1–5 Jas. 3. 13–end	Ps. 40 1 Kings 3. 1–15 Luke 20. 27–38	

		Sunday Principal Service Weekday Eucharist	Third Service Morning Prayer	Second Service Evening Prayer
7 Monday	**Willibrord of York, Bishop, Apostle of Frisia, 739**			
Rw *or* **Gw** **DEL 32**	Com. Missionary *or* *esp.* Isa. 52. 7–10 Matt. 28. 16–end	Titus 1. 1–9 Ps. 24. 1–6 Luke 17. 1–6	Ps. 19; **20** *alt.* Ps. **1**; 2; 3 Dan. 4. 19–end Rev. ch. 5	Ps. 34 alt. Ps. **4**; 7 Isa. 5. 8–24 Matt. 4.23 – 5.12
8 Tuesday	**The Saints and Martyrs of England**			
Rw *or* **Gw**	Isa. 61. 4–9 *or* Ecclus. 44. 1–15 Ps. 15 Rev. 19. 5–10 John 17. 18–23	*or* Titus 2. 1–8, 11–14 Ps. 37. 3–5, 30–32 Luke 17. 7–10	Ps. **21**; 24 *alt.* Ps. **5**; 6; (8) Dan. 5. 1–12 Rev. ch. 6	Ps. 36; **40** *alt.* Ps. **9**; 10† Isa. 5. 25–end Matt. 5. 13–20
9 Wednesday	*Margery Kempe, Mystic, c. 1440*			
R *or* **G**		Titus 3. 1–7 Ps. 23 Luke 17. 11–19	Ps. **23**; 25 *alt.* Ps. 119. 1–32 Dan. 5. 13–end Rev. 7. 1–4, 9–end	Ps. 37 *alt.* Ps. **11**; 12; 13 Isa. ch. 6 Matt. 5. 21–37
10 Thursday	**Leo the Great, Bishop of Rome, Teacher, 461**			
Rw *or* **Gw**	Com. Teacher *or* *also* 1 Pet. 5. 1–11	Philem. 7–20 Ps. 146. 4–end Luke 17. 20–25	Ps. **26**; 27 *alt.* Ps. 14; **15**; 16 Dan. ch. 6 Rev. ch. 8	Ps. 42; **43** *alt.* Ps. 18† Isa. 7. 1–17 Matt. 5. 38–end
11 Friday	**Martin, Bishop of Tours, c. 397**			
Rw *or* **Gw**	Com. Bishop *or* *also* 1 Thess. 5. 1–11 Matt. 25. 34–40	2 John 4–9 Ps. 119. 1–8 Luke 17. 26–end	Ps. 28; **32** *alt.* Ps. 17; **19** Dan. 7. 1–14 Rev. 9. 1–12	Ps. 31 *alt.* Ps. 22 Isa. 8. 1–15 Matt. 6. 1–18
12 Saturday				
R *or* **G**		3 John 5–8 Ps. 112 Luke 18. 1–8	Ps. 33 *alt.* Ps. 20; 21; **23** Dan. 7. 15–end Rev. 9. 13–end	Ps. 84; **86** *alt.* Ps. **24**; 25 Isa. 8.16 – 9.7 Matt. 6. 19–end ct
13 Sunday	**THE SECOND SUNDAY BEFORE ADVENT** (Remembrance Sunday)			
R *or* **G**		Mal. 4. 1–2a Ps. 98 2 Thess. 3. 6–13 Luke 21. 5–19	Ps. 132 1 Sam. 16. 1–13 Matt. 13. 44–52	Ps. [93]; 97 Dan. ch. 6 Matt. 13. 1–9, 18–23
14 Monday	*Samuel Seabury, first Anglican Bishop in North America, 1796*			
R *or* **G** **DEL 33**		Rev. 1. 1–4; 2. 1–5 Ps. 1 Luke 18. 35–end	Ps. 46; **47** *alt.* Ps. 27; **30** Dan. 8. 1–14 Rev. ch. 10	Ps. 70; **71** *alt.* Ps. 26; **28**; 29 Isa. 9.8 – 10.4 Matt. 7. 1–12
15 Tuesday				
R *or* **G**		Rev. 3. 1–6, 14–end Ps. 15 Luke 19. 1–10	Ps. 48; **52** *alt.* Ps. 32; **36** Dan. 8. 15–end Rev. 11. 1–14	Ps. **67**; 72 *alt.* Ps. 33 Isa. 10. 5–19 Matt. 7. 13–end

	Calendar and Holy Communion	Morning Prayer	Evening Prayer	NOTES
G		Dan. 4. 19–end Rev. ch. 5	Isa. 5. 8–24 Matt. 4.23 – 5.12	
G		Dan. 5. 1–12 Rev. ch. 6	Isa. 5. 25–end Matt. 5. 13–20	
G		Dan. 5. 13–end Rev. 7. 1–4, 9–end	Isa. ch. 6 Matt. 5. 21–37	
G		Dan. ch. 6 Rev. ch. 8	Isa. 7. 1–17 Matt. 5. 38–end	
	Martin, Bishop of Tours, c. 397			
Gw	Com. Bishop	Dan. 7. 1–14 Rev. 9. 1–12	Isa. 8. 1–15 Matt. 6. 1–18	
G		Dan. 7. 15–end Rev. 9. 13–end	Isa. 8.16 – 9.7 Matt. 6. 19–end	
			ct	
	THE TWENTY-SECOND SUNDAY AFTER TRINITY			
G	Gen. 45. 1–7, 15 Ps. 133 Phil. 1. 3–11 Matt. 18. 21–end	Ps. 132 1 Sam. 16. 1–13 Matt. 13. 44–52	Ps. [93]; 97 Dan. ch. 6 Matt. 13. 1–9, 18–23	
G		Dan. 8. 1–14 Rev. ch. 10	Isa. 9.8 – 10.4 Matt. 7. 1–12	
	Machutus, Bishop, Apostle of Brittany, c. 564			
Gw	Com. Bishop	Dan. 8. 15–end Rev. 11. 1–14	Isa. 10. 5–19 Matt. 7. 13–end	

		Sunday Principal Service / Weekday Eucharist	Third Service / Morning Prayer	Second Service / Evening Prayer
16 Wednesday	**Margaret, Queen of Scotland, Philanthropist, Reformer of the Church, 1093** *Edmund Rich of Abingdon, Archbishop of Canterbury, 1240*			
Rw *or* **Gw**	Com. Saint *or* *also* Prov. 31. 10–12, 20, 26–end 1 Cor. 12.13 – 13.3 Matt. 25. 34–end	Rev. ch. 4 Ps. 150 Luke 19. 11–28	Ps. *56*; 57 *alt.* Ps. 34 Dan. 9. 1–19 Rev. 11. 15–end	Ps. 73 *alt.* Ps. 119. 33–56 Isa. 10. 20–32 Matt. 8. 1–13
17 Thursday	**Hugh, Bishop of Lincoln, 1200**			
Rw *or* **Gw**	Com. Bishop *or* *also* 1 Tim. 6. 11–16	Rev. 5. 1–10 Ps. 149. 1–5 Luke 19. 41–44	Ps. 61; *62* *alt.* Ps. 37† Dan. 9. 20–end Rev. ch. 12	Ps. 74; *76* *alt.* Ps. 39; *40* Isa. 10.33 – 11.9 Matt. 8. 14–22
18 Friday	**Elizabeth of Hungary, Princess of Thuringia, Philanthropist, 1231**			
Rw *or* **Gw**	Com. Saint *or* *esp.* Matt. 25. 31–end *also* Prov. 31. 10–end	Rev. 10. 8–end Ps. 119. 65–72 Luke 19. 45–end	Ps. *63*; 65 *alt.* Ps. 31 Dan. 10.1 – 11.1 Rev. 13. 1–10	Ps. 77 *alt.* Ps. 35 Isa. 11.10 – 12.end Matt. 8. 23–end
19 Saturday	**Hilda, Abbess of Whitby, 680** *Mechtild, Béguine of Magdeburg, Mystic, 1280*			
Rw *or* **Gw**	Com. Religious *or* *esp.* Isa. 61.10 – 62.5	Rev. 11. 4–12 Ps. 144. 1–9 Luke 20. 27–40	Ps. 78. 1–39 *alt.* Ps. 41; *42*; 43 Dan. ch. 12 Rev. 13. 11–end	Ps. 78. 40–end *alt.* Ps. 45; *46* Isa. 13. 1–13 Matt. 9. 1–17 **ct** *or First EP of Christ* *the King* Ps. 99; 100 Isa. 10.33 – 11.9 1 Tim. 6. 11–16 **R** *or* **W ct**
20 Sunday	**CHRIST THE KING** The Sunday Next Before Advent			
R *or* **W**		Jer. 23. 1–6 Ps. 46 Col. 1. 11–20 Luke 23. 33–43	*MP*: Ps. 29; 110 Zech. 6. 9–end Rev. 11. 15–18	*EP*: Ps. 72 (or 72. 1–7) 1 Sam. 8. 4–20 John 18. 33–37
21 Monday				
R *or* **G** **DEL 34**		Rev. 14. 1–5 Ps. 24. 1–6 Luke 21. 1–4	Ps. 92; *96* *alt.* Ps. 44 Isa. 40. 1–11 Rev. 14. 1–13	Ps. 80; 81 *alt.* Ps. *47*; 49 Isa. 14. 3–20 Matt. 9. 18–34
22 Tuesday	*Cecilia, Martyr at Rome, c. 230*			
R *or* **G**		Rev. 14. 14–19 Ps. 96 Luke 21. 5–11	Ps. *97*; 98; 100 *alt.* Ps. *48*; 52 Isa. 40. 12–26 Rev. 14.14 – 15.end	Ps. 99; *101* *alt.* Ps. 50 Isa. ch. 17 Matt. 9.35 – 10.15
23 Wednesday	**Clement, Bishop of Rome, Martyr, c. 100**			
R *or* **Gr**	Com. Martyr *or* *also* Phil. 3.17 – 4.3 Matt. 16. 13–19	Rev. 15. 1–4 Ps. 98 Luke 21. 12–19	Ps. 110; 111; *112* *alt.* Ps. 119. 57–80 Isa. 40.27 – 41.7 Rev. 16. 1–11	Ps. 121; *122*; 123; 124 *alt.* Ps. *59*; 60; (67) Isa. ch. 19 Matt. 10. 16–33

	Calendar and Holy Communion	Morning Prayer	Evening Prayer	NOTES
G		Dan. 9. 1–19 Rev. 11. 15–end	Isa. 10. 20–32 Matt. 8. 1–13	
	Hugh, Bishop of Lincoln, 1200			
Gw	Com. Bishop	Dan. 9. 20–end Rev. ch. 12	Isa. 10.33 – 11.9 Matt. 8. 14–22	
G		Dan. 10.1 – 11.1 Rev. 13. 1–10	Isa. 11.10 – 12.end Matt. 8. 23–end	
G		Dan. ch. 12 Rev. 13. 11–end	Isa. 13. 1–13 Matt. 9. 1–17	

ct

THE SUNDAY NEXT BEFORE ADVENT
To celebrate Christ the King, see *Common Worship* provision.

	Calendar and Holy Communion	Morning Prayer	Evening Prayer	NOTES
G	Jer. 23. 5–8 Ps. 85. 8–end Col. 1. 13–20 John 6. 5–14	Ps. 29; 110 Zech. 6. 9–end Rev. 11. 15–18	Ps. 72 (or 72. 1–7) 1 Sam. 8. 4–20 John 18. 33–37	
G		Isa. 40. 1–11 Rev. 14. 1–13	Isa. 14. 3–20 Matt. 9. 18–34	
	Cecilia, Martyr at Rome, c. 230			
Gr	Com. Virgin Martyr	Isa. 40. 12–26 Rev. 14.14 – 15.end	Isa. ch. 17 Matt. 9.35 – 10.15	
	Clement, Bishop of Rome, Martyr, c. 100			
Gr	Com. Martyr	Isa. 40.27 – 41.7 Rev. 16. 1–11	Isa. ch. 19 Matt. 10. 16–33	

	Sunday Principal Service / Weekday Eucharist	Third Service / Morning Prayer	Second Service / Evening Prayer
24 Thursday			
R or **G**	Rev. 18. 1–2, 21–23; 19. 1–3, 9 Ps. 100 Luke 21. 20–28	Ps. *125*; 126; 127; 128 *alt.* Ps. 56; *57*; (63†) Isa. 41. 8–20 Rev. 16. 12–end	Ps. 131; 132; *133* *alt.* Ps. 61; *62*; 64 Isa. 21. 1–12 Matt. 10.34 – 11.1
25 Friday	*Catherine of Alexandria, Martyr, 4th century; Isaac Watts, Hymn Writer, 1748*		
R or **G**	Rev. 20.1–4, 11 – 21.2 Ps. 84. 1–6 Luke 21. 29–33	Ps. 139 *alt.* Ps. *51*; 54 Isa. 41.21 – 42.9 Rev. ch. 17	Ps. *146*; 147 *alt.* Ps. 38 Isa. 22. 1–14 Matt. 11. 2–19
26 Saturday			
R or **G**	Rev. 22. 1–7 Ps. 95. 1–7 Luke 21. 34–36	Ps. 145 *alt.* Ps. 68 Isa. 42. 10–17 Rev. ch. 18	Ps. 148; 149; *150* *alt.* Ps. 65; *66* Isa. ch. 24 Matt. 11. 20–end **P ct**
27 Sunday	**THE FIRST SUNDAY OF ADVENT** *Common Worship* Year A begins		
P	Isa. 2. 1–5 Ps. 122 Rom. 13. 11–end Matt. 24. 36–44	Ps. 44 Mic. 4. 1–7 1 Thess. 5. 1–11	Ps. 9 (or 9. 1–8) Isa. 52. 1–12 Matt. 24. 15–28
28 Monday	Daily Eucharistic Lectionary Year 1 begins		
P	Isa. 4. 2–end Ps. 122 Matt. 8. 5–11	Ps. *50*; 54 *alt.* Ps. *1*; 2; 3 Isa. 42. 18–end Rev. ch. 19	Ps. 70; *71* *alt.* Ps. *4*; 7 Isa. 25. 1–9 Matt. 12. 1–21
29 Tuesday			
P	Isa. 11. 1–10 Ps. 72. 1–4, 18–19 Luke 10. 21–24	Ps. *80*; 82 *alt.* Ps. *5*; 6; (8) Isa. 43. 1–13 Rev. ch. 20	Ps. *74*; 75 *alt.* Ps. *9*; 10† Isa. 26. 1–13 Matt. 12. 22–37 or *First EP of Andrew the Apostle* Ps. 48 Isa. 49. 1–9a 1 Cor. 4. 9–16 **R ct**
	Day of Intercession and Thanksgiving for the Missionary Work of the Church:		
	Isa. 49. 1–6; Isa. 52. 7–10; Mic. 4. 1–5 Ps. 2; 46; 47 Acts 17. 12–end; 2 Cor. 5.14 – 6.2; Eph. 2. 13–end Matt. 5. 13–16; Matt. 28. 16–end; John 17. 20–end		
30 Wednesday	**ANDREW THE APOSTLE**		
R	Isa. 52. 7–10 Ps. 19. 1–6 Rom. 10. 12–18 Matt. 4. 18–22	*MP*: Ps. 47; 147. 1–12 Ezek. 47. 1–12 or Ecclus. 14. 20–end John 12. 20–32	*EP*: Ps. 87; 96 Zech. 8. 20–end John 1. 35–42

	Calendar and Holy Communion	Morning Prayer	Evening Prayer	NOTES
G		Isa. 41. 8–20 Rev. 16. 12–end	Isa. 21. 1–12 Matt. 10.34 – 11.1	
	Catherine of Alexandria, Martyr, 4th century			
Gr	Com. Virgin Martyr	Isa. 41.21 – 42.9 Rev. ch. 17	Isa. 22. 1–14 Matt. 11. 2–19	
G		Isa. 42. 10–17 Rev. ch. 18	Isa. ch. 24 Matt. 11. 20–end	
			P ct	
	THE FIRST SUNDAY IN ADVENT Advent 1 Collect until Christmas Eve			
P	Mic. 4. 1–4, 6–7 Ps. 25. 1–9 Rom. 13. 8–14 Matt. 21. 1–13	Ps. 44 Isa. 2. 1–5 1 Thess. 5. 1–11	Ps. 9 (or 9. 1–8) Isa. 52. 1–12 Matt. 24. 15–28	
P		Isa. 42. 18–end Rev. ch. 19	Isa. 25. 1–9 Matt. 12. 1–21	
P		Isa. 43. 1–13 Rev. ch. 20	Isa. 26. 1–13 Matt. 12. 22–37 *or First EP of Andrew the Apostle* (Ps. 48) Isa. 49. 1–9a 1 Cor. 4. 9–16	
			R ct	

To celebrate the Day of Intercession and Thanksgiving for the Missionary Work of the Church, see *Common Worship* provision.

	ANDREW THE APOSTLE			
R	Zech. 8. 20–end Ps. 92. 1–5 Rom. 10. 9–end Matt. 4. 18–22	(Ps. 47; 147. 1–12) Ezek. 47. 1–12 *or* Ecclus. 14. 20–end John 12. 20–32	(Ps. 87; 96) Isa. 52. 7–10 John 1. 35–42	

		Sunday Principal Service Weekday Eucharist	Third Service Morning Prayer	Second Service Evening Prayer

December 2022

---

1 Thursday   *Charles de Foucauld, Hermit in the Sahara, 1916*

P		Isa. 26. 1–6 Ps. 118. 18–27a Matt. 7. 21, 24–27	Ps. *42*; 43 *alt.* Ps. 14; *15*; 16 Isa. 44. 1–8 Rev. 21. 9–21	Ps. *40*; 46 *alt.* Ps. 18† Isa. 28. 14–end Matt. 13. 1–23

---

2 Friday

P		Isa. 29. 17–end Ps. 27. 1–4, 16–17 Matt. 9. 27–31	Ps. *25*; 26 *alt.* Ps. 17; *19* Isa. 44. 9–23 Rev. 21.22 – 22.5	Ps. 16; *17* *alt.* Ps. 22 Isa. 29. 1–14 Matt. 13. 24–43

---

3 Saturday   *Francis Xavier, Missionary, Apostle of the Indies, 1552*

P		Isa. 30. 19–21, 23–26 Ps. 146. 4–9 Matt. 9.35 – 10.1, 6–8	Ps. *9*; (10) *alt.* Ps. 20; 21; *23* Isa. 44.24 – 45.13 Rev. 22. 6–end	Ps. *27*; 28 *alt.* Ps. *24*; 25 Isa. 29. 15–end Matt. 13. 44–end **ct**

---

4 Sunday   **THE SECOND SUNDAY OF ADVENT**

P		Isa. 11. 1–10 Ps. 72. 1–7, 18–19 (or 72. 1–7) Rom. 15. 4–13 Matt. 3. 1–12	Ps. 80 Amos ch. 7 Luke 1. 5–20	Ps. 11; [28] 1 Kings 18. 17–39 John 1. 19–28

---

5 Monday

P		Isa. ch. 35 Ps. 85. 7–end Luke 5. 17–26	Ps. 44 *alt.* Ps. 27; *30* Isa. 45. 14–end 1 Thess. ch. 1	Ps. *144*; 146 *alt.* Ps. 26; *28*; 29 Isa. 30. 1–18 Matt. 14. 1–12

---

6 Tuesday   **Nicholas, Bishop of Myra, c. 326**

Pw	Com. Bishop *also* Isa. 61. 1–3 1 Tim. 6. 6–11 Mark 10. 13–16	*or* Isa. 40. 1–11 Ps. 96. 1, 10–end Matt. 18. 12–14	Ps. *56*; 57 *alt.* Ps. 32; *36* Isa. ch. 46 1 Thess. 2. 1–12	Ps. *11*; 12; 13 *alt.* Ps. 33 Isa. 30. 19–end Matt. 14. 13–end

---

7 Wednesday   **Ambrose, Bishop of Milan, Teacher, 397**
Ember Day*

Pw	Com. Teacher *also* Isa. 41. 9b–13 Luke 22. 24–30	*or* Isa. 40. 25–end Ps. 103. 8–13 Matt. 11. 28–end	Ps. *62*; 63 *alt.* Ps. 34 Isa. ch. 47 1 Thess. 2. 13–end	Ps. *10*; 14 *alt.* Ps. 119. 33–56 Isa. ch. 31 Matt. 15. 1–20

---

8 Thursday   **The Conception of the Blessed Virgin Mary**

Pw	Com. BVM	*or* Isa. 41. 13–20 Ps. 145. 1, 8–13 Matt. 11. 11–15	Ps. 53; *54*; 60 *alt.* Ps. 37† Isa. 48. 1–11 1 Thess. ch. 3	Ps. 73 *alt.* Ps. 39; *40* Isa. ch. 32 Matt. 15. 21–28

---

9 Friday   Ember Day*

P		Isa. 48. 17–19 Ps. 1 Matt. 11. 16–19	Ps. 85; *86* *alt.* Ps. 31 Isa. 48. 12–end 1 Thess. 4. 1–12	Ps. 82; *90* *alt.* Ps. 35 Isa. 33. 1–22 Matt. 15. 29–end

---

*For Ember Day provision, see p. 11.

	Calendar and Holy Communion	Morning Prayer	Evening Prayer	NOTES
P		Isa. 44. 1–8 Rev. 21. 9–21	Isa. 28. 14–end Matt. 13. 1–23	
P		Isa. 44. 9–23 Rev. 21.22 – 22.5	Isa. 29. 1–14 Matt. 13. 24–43	
P		Isa. 44.24 – 45.13 Rev. 22. 6–end	Isa. 29. 15–end Matt. 13. 44–end	
			ct	
THE SECOND SUNDAY IN ADVENT				
P	2 Kings 22. 8–10; 23. 1–3 Ps. 50. 1–6 Rom. 15. 4–13 Luke 21. 25–33	Ps. 80 Amos ch. 7 Luke 1. 5–20	Ps. 11; [28] 1 Kings 18. 17–39 Matt. 3. 1–12	
P		Isa. 45. 14–end 1 Thess. ch. 1	Isa. 30. 1–18 Matt. 14. 1–12	
Nicholas, Bishop of Myra, c. 326				
Pw	Com. Bishop	Isa. ch. 46 1 Thess. 2. 1–12	Isa. 30. 19–end Matt. 14. 13–end	
P		Isa. ch. 47 1 Thess. 2. 13–end	Isa. ch. 31 Matt. 15. 1–20	
The Conception of the Blessed Virgin Mary				
Pw		Isa. 48. 1–11 1 Thess. ch. 3	Isa. ch. 32 Matt. 15. 21–28	
P		Isa. 48. 12–end 1 Thess. 4. 1–12	Isa. 33. 1–22 Matt. 15. 29–end	

		Sunday Principal Service Weekday Eucharist	Third Service Morning Prayer	Second Service Evening Prayer
10 Saturday	Ember Day*			
P		Ecclus. 48. 1–4, 9–11 *or* 2 Kings 2. 9–12 Ps. 80. 1–4, 18–19 Matt. 17. 10–13	Ps. 145 *alt.* Ps. 41; **42**; 43 Isa. 49. 1–13 1 Thess. 4. 13–end	Ps. 93; **94** *alt.* Ps. 45; **46** Isa. ch. 35 Matt. 16. 1–12 **ct**
11 Sunday	**THE THIRD SUNDAY OF ADVENT**			
P		Isa. 35. 1–10 Ps. 146. 4–10 *or Canticle*: Magnificat Jas. 5. 7–10 Matt. 11. 2–11	Ps. 68. 1–19 Zeph. 3. 14–end Phil. 4. 4–7	Ps. 12; [14] Isa. 5. 8–end Acts 13. 13–41 *Gospel*: John 5. 31–40
12 Monday				
P		Num. 24. 2–7, 15–17 Ps. 25. 3–8 Matt. 21. 23–27	Ps. 40 *alt.* Ps. 44 Isa. 49. 14–25 1 Thess. 5. 1–11	Ps. 25; **26** *alt.* Ps. **47**; 49 Isa. 38. 1–8, 21–22 Matt. 16. 13–end
13 Tuesday	**Lucy, Martyr at Syracuse, 304** *Samuel Johnson, Moralist, 1784*			
Pr		Com. Martyr *or* Zeph. 3. 1–2, 9–13 *also* Wisd. 3. 1–7 Ps. 34. 1–6, 21–22 2 Cor. 4. 6–15 Matt. 21. 28–32	Ps. **70**; 74 *alt.* Ps. **48**; 52 Isa. ch. 50 1 Thess. 5. 12–end	Ps. **50**; 54 *alt.* Ps. 50 Isa. 38. 9–20 Matt. 17. 1–13
14 Wednesday	**John of the Cross, Poet, Teacher, 1591**			
Pw		Com. Teacher *or* Isa. 45. 6b–8, 18, *esp.* 1 Cor. 2. 1–10 21b–end *also* John 14. 18–23 Ps. 85. 7–end Luke 7. 18b–23	Ps. **75**; 96 *alt.* Ps. 119. 57–80 Isa. 51. 1–8 2 Thess. ch. 1	Ps. 25; **82** *alt.* Ps. **59**; 60; (67) Isa. ch. 39 Matt. 17. 14–21
15 Thursday				
P		Isa. 54. 1–10 Ps. 30. 1–5, 11–end Luke 7. 24–30	Ps. **76**; 97 *alt.* Ps. 56; **57**; (63†) Isa. 51. 9–16 2 Thess. ch. 2	Ps. 44 *alt.* Ps. 61; **62**; 64 Zeph. 1.1 – 2.3 Matt. 17. 22–end
16 Friday				
P		Isa. 56. 1–3a, 6–8 Ps. 67 John 5. 33–36	Ps. 77; **98** *alt.* Ps. **51**; 54 Isa. 51. 17–end 2 Thess. ch. 3	Ps. 49 *alt.* Ps. 38 Zeph. 3. 1–13 Matt. 18. 1–20
17 Saturday	O Sapientia *Eglantyne Jebb, Social Reformer, Founder of 'Save the Children', 1928*			
P		Gen. 49. 2, 8–10 Ps. 72. 1–5, 18–19 Matt. 1. 1–17	Ps. 71 *alt.* Ps. 68 Isa. 52. 1–12 Jude	Ps. 42; **43** *alt.* Ps. 65; **66** Zeph. 3. 14–end Matt. 18. 21–end **ct**
18 Sunday	**THE FOURTH SUNDAY OF ADVENT**			
P		Isa. 7. 10–16 Ps. 80. 1–8, 18–20 (*or* 80. 1–8) Rom. 1. 1–7 Matt. 1. 18–end	Ps. 144 Mic. 5. 2–5a Luke 1. 26–38	Ps. 113; [126] 1 Sam. 1. 1–20 Rev. 22. 6–end *Gospel*: Luke 1. 39–45

*For Ember Day provision, see p. 11.

	Calendar and Holy Communion	Morning Prayer	Evening Prayer	NOTES
P		Isa. 49. 1–13 1 Thess. 4. 13–end	Isa. ch. 35 Matt. 16. 1–12	
			ct	

THE THIRD SUNDAY IN ADVENT

	Calendar and Holy Communion	Morning Prayer	Evening Prayer	NOTES
P	Isa. ch. 35 Ps. 80. 1–7 1 Cor. 4. 1–5 Matt. 11. 2–10	Ps. 68. 1–19 Zeph. 3. 14–end Jas. 5. 7–10	Ps. 12; [14] Isa. 5. 8–end Acts 13. 13–41	
P		Isa. 49. 14–25 1 Thess. 5. 1–11	Isa. 38. 1–8, 21–22 Matt. 16. 13–end	

	Lucy, Martyr at Syracuse, 304			
Pr	Com. Virgin Martyr	Isa. ch. 50 1 Thess. 5. 12–end	Isa. 38. 9–20 Matt. 17. 1–13	

	Ember Day			
P	Ember CEG	Isa. 51. 1–8 2 Thess. ch. 1	Isa. ch. 39 Matt. 17. 14–21	
P		Isa. 51. 9–16 2 Thess. ch. 2	Zeph. 1.1 – 2.3 Matt. 17. 22–end	

	O Sapientia Ember Day			
P	Ember CEG	Isa. 51. 17–end 2 Thess. ch. 3	Zeph. 3. 1–13 Matt. 18. 1–20	

	Ember Day			
P	Ember CEG	Isa. 52. 1–12 Jude	Zeph. 3. 14–end Matt. 18. 21–end	
			ct	

THE FOURTH SUNDAY IN ADVENT

	Calendar and Holy Communion	Morning Prayer	Evening Prayer	NOTES
P	Isa. 40. 1–9 Ps. 145. 17–end Phil. 4. 4–7 John 1. 19–28	Ps. 144 Mic. 5. 2–5a Luke 1. 26–38	Ps. 113; [126] 1 Sam. 1. 1–20 Rev. 22. 6–end	

	Sunday Principal Service Weekday Eucharist	Third Service Morning Prayer	Second Service Evening Prayer

19 Monday

P	Judg. 13. 2–7, 24–end Ps. 71. 3–8 Luke 1. 5–25	Ps. 144; *146* Isa. 52.13 – 53.end 2 Pet. 1. 1–15	Ps. 10; *57* Mal. 1. 1, 6–end Matt. 19. 1–12

20 Tuesday

P	Isa. 7. 10–14 Ps. 24. 1–6 Luke 1. 26–38	Ps. *46*; 95 Isa. ch. 54 2 Pet. 1.16 – 2.3	Ps. *4*; 9 Mal. 2. 1–16 Matt. 19. 13–15

21 Wednesday*

P	Zeph. 3. 14–18 Ps. 33. 1–4, 11–12, 20–end Luke 1. 39–45	Ps. *121*; 122; 123 Isa. ch. 55 2 Pet. 2. 4–end	Ps. 80; *84* Mal. 2.17 – 3.12 Matt. 19. 16–end

22 Thursday

P	1 Sam. 1. 24–end Ps. 113 Luke 1. 46–56	Ps. *124*; 125; 126; 127 Isa. 56. 1–8 2 Pet. ch. 3	Ps. 24; *48* Mal. 3.13 – 4.end Matt. 23. 1–12

23 Friday

P	Mal. 3. 1–4; 4. 5–end Ps. 25. 3–9 Luke 1. 57–66	Ps. 128; 129; *130*; 131 Isa. 63. 1–6 2 John	Ps. 89. 1–37 Nahum ch. 1 Matt. 23. 13–28

24 Saturday   **CHRISTMAS EVE**

P	*Morning Eucharist* 2 Sam. 7. 1–5, 8–11, 16 Ps. 89. 2, 19–27 Acts 13. 16–26 Luke 1. 67–79	Ps. *45*; 113 Isa. ch. 58 3 John	Ps. 85 Zech. ch. 2 Rev. 1. 1–8

25 Sunday   **CHRISTMAS DAY**

w	*Any of the following sets of readings may be used on the evening of Christmas Eve and on Christmas Day. Set III should be used at some service during the celebration.*	*I* Isa. 9. 2–7 Ps. 96 Titus 2. 11–14 Luke 2. 1–14 [15–20] *II* Isa. 62. 6–end Ps. 97 Titus 3. 4–7 Luke 2. [1–7] 8–20 *III* Isa. 52. 7–10 Ps. 98 Heb. 1. 1–4 [5–12] John 1. 1–14	MP: Ps. *110*; 117 Isa. 62. 1–5 Matt. 1. 18–end	*EP*: Ps. 8 Isa. 65. 17–25 Phil. 2. 5–11 *or* Luke 2. 1–20 *if it has not been used at the principal service of the day*

*Thomas the Apostle may be celebrated on 21 December instead of 3 July.

	Calendar and Holy Communion	Morning Prayer	Evening Prayer	NOTES
P		Isa. 52.13 – 53.end 2 Pet. 1. 1–15	Mal. 1. 1, 6–end Matt. 19. 1–12	
P		Isa. ch. 54 2 Pet. 1.16 – 2.3	Mal. 2. 1–16 Matt. 19. 13–15 *or First EP of Thomas* (Ps. 27) Isa. ch. 35 Heb. 10.35 – 11.1 **R ct**	
	THOMAS THE APOSTLE			
R	Job 42. 1–6 Ps. 139. 1–11 Eph. 2. 19–end John 20. 24–end	(Ps. 92; 146) 2 Sam. 15. 17–21 *or* Ecclus. ch. 2 John 11. 1–16	(Ps. 139) Hab. 2. 1–4 1 Pet. 1. 3–12	
P		Isa. 56. 1–8 2 Pet. ch. 3	Mal. 3.13 – 4.end Matt. 23. 1–12	
P		Isa. 63. 1–6 2 John	Nahum ch. 1 Matt. 23. 13–28	
	CHRISTMAS EVE			
P	Collect (1) Christmas Eve (2) Advent 1 Mic. 5. 2–5a Ps. 24 Titus 3. 3–7 Luke 2. 1–14	Isa. ch. 58 3 John	Zech. ch. 2 Rev. 1. 1–8	
	CHRISTMAS DAY			
𝖜	Isa. 9. 2–7 Ps. 98 Heb. 1. 1–12 John 1. 1–14	Ps. 110; 117 Isa. 62. 1–5 Matt. 1. 18–end	Ps. 8 Isa. 65. 17–25 Phil. 2. 5–11 *or* Luke 2. 1–20	

	Sunday Principal Service Weekday Eucharist	Third Service Morning Prayer	Second Service Evening Prayer

---

26 Monday   **STEPHEN, DEACON, FIRST MARTYR**

R	2 Chron. 24. 20–22 or Acts 7. 51–end Ps. 119. 161–168 Acts 7. 51–end or Gal. 2. 16b–20 Matt. 10. 17–22	MP: Ps. **13**; 31. 1–8; 150 Jer. 26. 12–15 Acts ch. 6	EP: Ps. 57; **86** Gen. 4. 1–10 Matt. 23. 34–end

---

27 Tuesday   **JOHN, APOSTLE AND EVANGELIST**

W	Exod. 33. 7–11a Ps. 117 1 John ch. 1 John 21. 19b–end	MP: Ps. **21**; 147. 13–end Exod. 33. 12–end 1 John 2. 1–11	EP: Ps. 97 Isa. 6. 1–8 1 John 5. 1–12

---

28 Wednesday   **THE HOLY INNOCENTS**

R	Jer. 31. 15–17 Ps. 124 1 Cor. 1. 26–29 Matt. 2. 13–18	MP: Ps. **36**; 146 Baruch 4. 21–27 or Gen. 37. 13–20 Matt. 18. 1–10	EP: Ps. 123; **128** Isa. 49. 14–25 Mark 10. 13–16

---

29 Thursday   **Thomas Becket, Archbishop of Canterbury, Martyr, 1170***

Wr	Com. Martyr or esp. Matt. 10. 28–33 also Ecclus. 51. 1–8	1 John 2. 3–11 Ps. 96. 1–4 Luke 2. 22–35	Ps. **19**; 20 Isa. 57. 15–end John 1. 1–18	Ps. 131; **132** Jonah ch. 1 Col. 1. 1–14

30 Friday

W		1 John 2. 12–17 Ps. 96. 7–10 Luke 2. 36–40	Ps. 111; 112; **113** Isa. 59. 1–15a John 1. 19–28	Ps. **65**; 84 Jonah ch. 2 Col. 1. 15–23

31 Saturday   *John Wyclif, Reformer, 1384*

W		1 John 2. 18–21 Ps. 96. 1, 11–end John 1. 1–18	Ps. 102 Isa. 59. 15b–end John 1. 29–34	Ps. **90**; 148 Jonah chs 3 & 4 Col. 1.24 – 2.7 or First EP of The Naming of Jesus Ps. 148 Jer. 23. 1–6 Col. 2. 8–15 **ct**

*Thomas Becket may be celebrated on 7 July instead of 29 December.

	Calendar and Holy Communion	Morning Prayer	Evening Prayer	NOTES
	STEPHEN, DEACON, FIRST MARTYR			
R	Collect (1) Stephen (2) Christmas 2 Chron. 24. 20–22 Ps. 119. 161–168 Acts 7. 55–end Matt. 23. 34–end	(Ps. 13; 31. 1–8; 150) Jer. 26. 12–15 Acts ch. 6	(Ps. 57; 86) Gen. 4. 1–10 Matt. 10. 17–22	
	JOHN, APOSTLE AND EVANGELIST			
W	Collect (1) John (2) Christmas Exod. 33. 18–end Ps. 92. 11–end 1 John ch. 1 John 21. 19b–end	(Ps. 21; 147. 13–end) Exod. 33. 7–11a 1 John 2. 1–11	(Ps. 97) Isa. 6. 1–8 1 John 5. 1–12	
	THE HOLY INNOCENTS			
R	Collect (1) Innocents (2) Christmas Jer. 31. 10–17 Ps. 123 Rev. 14. 1–5 Matt. 2. 13–18	(Ps. 36; 146) Baruch 4. 21–27 or Gen. 37. 13–20 Matt. 18. 1–10	(Ps. 124; 128) Isa. 49. 14–25 Mark 10. 13–16	
W	CEG of Christmas	Isa. 57. 15–end John 1. 1–18	Jonah ch. 1 Col. 1. 1–14	
W		Isa. 59. 1–15a John 1. 19–28	Jonah ch. 2 Col. 1. 15–23	
	Silvester, Bishop of Rome, 335			
W	Com. Bishop	Isa. 59. 15b–end John 1. 29–34	Jonah chs 3 & 4 Col. 1.24 – 2.7 or First EP of The Circumcision of Christ Ps. 148 Jer. 23. 1–6 Col. 2. 8–15	

ct

The *Common Worship* Additional Weekday Lectionary

The Additional Weekday Lectionary provides two readings on a one-year cycle for each day (except for Sundays, Principal Feasts and Holy Days, Festivals and Holy Week). They 'stand alone' and are intended particularly for use in those churches and cathedrals that attract occasional rather than regular congregations. The Additional Weekday Lectionary has been designed to complement rather than replace the existing Weekday Lectionary. Thus a church with a regular congregation in the morning and a congregation made up mainly of visitors in the evening would continue to use the Weekday Lectionary in the morning but might choose to use this Additional Weekday Lectionary for Evening Prayer.

Psalms are not provided, since the Weekday Lectionary already offers a variety of approaches with regard to psalmody. This Lectionary is not intended for use at the Eucharist; the Daily Eucharistic Lectionary is already authorized for that purpose.

On Sundays, Principal Feasts, other Principal Holy Days, Festivals, and in Holy Week, where no readings are provided in this table, the lectionary provision in the main part of this volume should be used.

Date		Old Testament	New Testament
November 2021			
28	S	THE FIRST SUNDAY OF ADVENT	
29	M	Mal. 3. 1–6	Matt. 3. 1–6
30	Tu	ANDREW	
December 2021			
1	W	Isa. 65.17 – 66.2	Matt. 24. 1–14
2	Th	Mic. 5. 2–5a	John 3. 16–21
3	F	Isa. 66. 18–end	Luke 13. 22–30
4	Sa	Mic. 7. 8–15	Rom. 15.30 – 16.7, 25–end
5	S	THE SECOND SUNDAY OF ADVENT	
6	M	Jer. 7. 1–11	Phil. 4. 4–9
7	Tu	Dan. 7. 9–14	Matt. 24. 15–28
8	W	Amos 9. 11–end	Rom. 13. 8–end
9	Th	Jer. 23. 5–8	Mark 11. 1–11
10	F	Jer. 33. 14–22	Luke 21. 25–36
11	Sa	Zech. 14. 4–11	Rev. 22. 1–7
12	S	THE THIRD SUNDAY OF ADVENT	
13	M	Isa. 40. 1–11	Matt. 3. 1–12
14	Tu	Lam. 3. 22–33	1 Cor. 1. 1–9
15	W	Joel 3. 9–16	Matt. 24. 29–35
16	Th	Isa. ch. 62	1 Thess. 3. 6–13
17	F	Ecclus. 24. 1–9 or Prov. 6. 22–31	1 Cor. 2. 1–13
18	Sa	Exod. 3. 1–6	Acts 7. 20–36
19	S	THE FOURTH SUNDAY OF ADVENT	
20	M	Isa. 22. 21–23	Rev. 3. 7–13
21	Tu	Num. 24. 15b–19	Rev. 22. 10–21
22	W	Jer. 30. 7–11a	Acts 4. 1–12
23	Th	Isa. 7. 10–15	Matt. 1. 18–23
24	F	At Evening Prayer, the readings for Christmas Eve are used. At other services, the following readings are used:	
		Isa. 29. 13–18	1 John 4. 7–16
25	Sa	**CHRISTMAS DAY**	
26	S	STEPHEN (or transferred to 29th) or THE FIRST SUNDAY OF CHRISTMAS	
27	M	JOHN THE EVANGELIST	
28	Tu	THE HOLY INNOCENTS	
29	W	Mic. 1. 1–4; 2. 12–13	Luke 2. 1–7
30	Th	Isa. 9. 2–7	John 8. 12–20
31	F	Eccles. 3. 1–13	Rev. 21. 1–8
January 2022			
1	Sa	**NAMING AND CIRCUMCISION OF JESUS**	
2	S	THE SECOND SUNDAY OF CHRISTMAS (or The Epiphany)	
3	M	Deut. 6. 4–15	John 10. 31–end
		Where, for pastoral reasons, The Epiphany is celebrated on Sunday 2 January, the following readings are used:	
		Isa. 66. 6–14	Matt. 12. 46–50
4	Tu	Isa. 63. 7–16	Gal. 3.23 – 4.7
		Where, for pastoral reasons, The Epiphany is celebrated on Sunday 2 January, the following readings are used:	

Date		Old Testament	New Testament
		Deut. 6. 4–15	John 10. 31–end
5	W	At Evening prayer, the readings for the Eve of Epiphany are used. At other services, the following readings are used:	
		Isa. ch. 12	2 Cor. 2. 12–end
		Where, for pastoral reasons, The Epiphany is celebrated on Sunday 2 January, the following readings are used:	
		Isa. 63. 7–16	Gal. 3.23 – 4.7
6	Th	**THE EPIPHANY**	
		Where, for pastoral reasons, The Epiphany is celebrated on Sunday 2 January, the following readings are used:	
		Isa. ch. 12	2 Cor. 2. 12–end
7	F	Gen. 25. 19–end	Eph. 1. 1–6
8	Sa	At Evening Prayer, the readings for the Eve of The Baptism of Christ are used. At other services, the following readings are used:	
		Joel 2. 28–end	Eph. 1. 7–14
9	S	THE BAPTISM OF CHRIST (The First Sunday of Epiphany)	
10	M	Isa. 41. 14–20	John 1. 29–34
11	Tu	Exod. 17. 1–7	Acts 8. 26–end
12	W	Exod. 15. 1–19	Col. 2. 8–15
13	Th	Zech. 6. 9–15	1 Pet. 2. 4–10
14	F	Isa. 51. 7–16	Gal. 6. 14–18
15	Sa	Lev. 16. 11–22	Heb. 10. 19–25
16	S	THE SECOND SUNDAY OF EPIPHANY	
17	M	1 Kings. 17. 8–16	Mark 8. 1–10
18	Tu	1 Kings 19. 1–9a	Mark 1. 9–15
19	W	1 Kings 19. 9b–18	Mark 9. 2–13
20	Th	Lev. 11. 1–8, 13–19, 41–45	Acts 10. 9–16
21	F	Isa. 49. 8–13	Acts 10. 34–43
22	Sa	Gen. 35. 1–15	Acts 10. 44–end
23	S	THE THIRD SUNDAY OF EPIPHANY	
24	M	Ezek. 37. 15–end	John 17. 1–19
25	Tu	THE CONVERSION OF PAUL	
26	W	Neh. 2. 1–10	Rom. 12. 1–8
27	Th	Deut. 26. 16–end	Rom. 14. 1–9
28	F	Lev. 19. 9–28	Rom. 15. 1–7
29	Sa	Jer. 33. 1–11	1 Pet. 5. 5b–end
		or, where The Presentation is celebrated on Sunday 30 January, First EP of The Presentation of Christ	
30	S	THE FOURTH SUNDAY OF EPIPHANY (or The Presentation)	
31	M	Jonah ch. 3	2 Cor. 5. 11–21
February 2022			
1	Tu	At Evening Prayer, the readings for the Eve of The Presentation are used. At other services, the following readings are used:	
		Prov. 4. 10–end	Matt. 5. 13–20
2	W	**THE PRESENTATION** or	
		Isa. 61. 1–9	Luke 7. 18–30
3	Th	Isa. 52. 1–12	Matt. 10. 1–15
4	F	Isa. 56. 1–8	Matt. 28. 16–end
5	Sa	Hab. 2. 1–4	Rev. 14. 1–7

6	S	THE FOURTH SUNDAY BEFORE LENT	
7	M	Gen. 1. 26–end	Matt. 10. 1–16
8	Tu	Ruth 1. 1–18	1 John 3. 14–end
9	W	1 Sam. 1. 19b–end	Luke 2. 41–end
10	Th	Gen. 47. 1–12	Eph. 3. 14–end
11	F	2 Sam. 1. 17–end	Rom. 8. 28–end
12	Sa	Song of Sol. 2. 8–end	1 Cor. ch. 13
13	S	THE THIRD SUNDAY BEFORE LENT	
14	M	Exod. 23. 1–13	Jas. 2. 1–13
15	Tu	Deut. 10. 12–end	Heb. 13. 1–16
16	W	Isa. 58. 6–end	Matt. 25. 31–end
17	Th	Isa. 42. 1–9	Luke 4. 14–21
18	F	Amos 5. 6–15	Eph. 4. 25–end
19	Sa	Amos 5. 18–24	John 2. 13–22
20	S	THE SECOND SUNDAY BEFORE LENT	
21	M	Isa. 61. 1–9	Mark 6. 1–13
22	Tu	Isa. 52. 1–10	Rom. 10. 5–21
23	W	Isa. 52.13 – 53.6	Rom. 15. 14–21
24	Th	Isa. 53. 4–12	2 Cor. 4. 1–10
25	F	Zech. 8. 16–end	Matt. 10. 1–15
26	Sa	Jer. 1. 4–10	Matt. 10. 16–22
27	S	THE SUNDAY NEXT BEFORE LENT	
28	M	2 Kings 2. 13–22	3 John

March 2022

1	Tu	Judg. 14. 5–17	Rev. 10. 4–11
2	W	**ASH WEDNESDAY**	
3	Th	Gen. 2. 7–end	Heb. 2. 5–end
4	F	Gen. 4. 1–12	Heb. 4. 12–end
5	Sa	2 Kings 22. 11–end	Heb. 5. 1–10
6	S	THE FIRST SUNDAY OF LENT	
7	M	Gen. 6. 11–end; 7. 11–16	Luke 4. 14–21
8	Tu	Deut. 31. 7–13	1 John 3. 1–10
9	W	Gen. 11. 1–9	Matt. 24. 15–28
10	Th	Gen. 31. 1–13	1 Pet. 2. 13–end
11	F	Gen. 21. 1–8	Luke 9. 18–27
12	Sa	Gen. 32. 22–32	2 Pet. 1. 10–end
13	S	THE SECOND SUNDAY OF LENT	
14	M	1 Chron. 21. 1–17	1 John 2. 1–8
15	Tu	Zech. ch. 3	2 Pet. 2. 1–10a
16	W	Job. 1. 1–22	Luke 21.34 – 22.6
17	Th	2 Chron. 29. 1–11	Mark 11. 15–19
18	F	Exod. 19. 1–9a	1 Pet. 1. 1–9
19	Sa	JOSEPH OF NAZARETH	
20	S	THE THIRD SUNDAY OF LENT	
21	M	Josh. 4. 1–13	Luke 9. 1–11
22	Tu	Exod. 15. 22–27	Heb. 10. 32–end
23	W	Gen. 9. 8–17	1 Pet. 3. 18–end
24	Th	*At Evening Prayer, the readings for the Eve of The Annunciation are used. At other services, the following readings are used:*	
		Dan. 12. 5–end	Mark 13. 21–end
25	F	**THE ANNUNCIATION**	
26	Sa	Isa. 43. 14–end	Heb. 3. 1–15
27	S	THE FOURTH SUNDAY OF LENT **(Mothering Sunday)**	
28	M	2 Kings 24.18 – 25.7	1 Cor. 15. 20–34
29	Tu	Jer. 13. 12–19	Acts 13. 26–35
30	W	Jer. 13. 20–27	1 Pet. 1.17 – 2.3
31	Th	Jer. 22. 11–19	Luke 11. 37–52

April 2022

1	F	Jer. 17. 1–14	Luke 6. 17–26
2	Sa	Ezra ch. 1	2 Cor. 1. 12–19
3	S	THE FIFTH SUNDAY OF LENT **(Passiontide begins)**	
4	M	Joel 2. 12–17	2 John
5	Tu	Isa. 58. 1–14	Mark 10. 32–45
6	W	Joel 36. 1–12	John 14. 1–14
7	Th	Jer. 9. 17–22	Luke 13. 31–35
8	F	Lam. 5. 1–3, 19–22	John 12. 20–26
9	Sa	Job 17. 6–end	John 12. 27–36
10	S	PALM SUNDAY	
		HOLY WEEK	

17	S	**EASTER DAY**	
18	M	Isa. 54. 1–14	Rom. 1. 1–7
19	Tu	Isa. 51. 1–11	John 5. 19–29
20	W	Isa. 26. 1–19	John 20. 1–10
21	Th	Isa. 43. 14–21	Rev. 1. 4–end
22	F	Isa. 42. 10–17	1 Thess. 5. 1–11
23	Sa	Job 14. 1–14	John 21. 1–14
24	S	THE SECOND SUNDAY OF EASTER	
25	M	MARK	
26	Tu	GEORGE (transferred from 23 April)	
27	W	Hos. 5.15 – 6.6	1 Cor. 15. 1–11
28	Th	Jonah ch. 2	Mark 4. 35–end
29	F	Gen. 6. 9–end	1 Pet. 3. 8–end
30	Sa	1 Sam. 2. 1–8	Matt. 28. 8–15

May 2022

1	S	THE THIRD SUNDAY OF EASTER	
2	M	PHILIP AND JAMES (transferred from 1 May)	
3	Tu	Lev. 19. 9–18, 32–end	Matt. 5. 38–end
4	W	Gen. 3. 8–21	1 Cor. 15. 12–28
5	Th	Isa. 33. 13–22	Mark 6. 47–end
6	F	Neh. 9. 6–17	Rom. 5. 12–end
7	Sa	Isa. 61.10 – 62.5	Luke 24. 1–12
8	S	THE FOURTH SUNDAY OF EASTER	
9	M	Jer. 31. 10–17	Rev. 7. 9–end
10	Tu	Job 31. 13–23	Matt. 7. 1–12
11	W	Gen. 2. 4b–9	1 Cor. 15. 35–49
12	Th	Prov. 28. 3–end	Mark 10. 17–31
13	F	Eccles. 12. 1–8	Rom. 6. 1–11
14	Sa	MATTHIAS	
		Where Matthias is celebrated on 24 February:	
		1 Chron. 29. 10–13	Luke 24. 13–35
15	S	THE FIFTH SUNDAY OF EASTER	
16	M	Gen. 5. 1–18	Rom. 4. 13–end
17	Tu	Deut. 8. 1–10	Matt. 6. 19–end
18	W	Hos. 13. 4–14	1 Cor. 15. 50–end
19	Th	Gen. 3. 1–15	Mark 12. 18–27
20	F	Ezek. 36. 33–end	Rom. 8. 1–11
21	Sa	Isa. 38. 9–20	Luke 24. 33–end
22	S	THE SIXTH SUNDAY OF EASTER	
23	M	Prov. 4. 1–13	Phil. 2. 1–11
24	Tu	Isa. 32. 12–end	Rom. 5. 1–11
25	W	*At Evening Prayer, the readings for the Eve of Ascension Day are used. At other services, the following readings are used:*	
		Isa. 43. 1–13	Titus 2.11 – 3.8
26	Th	**ASCENSION DAY**	
27	F	Exod. 35.30 – 36.1	Gal. 5. 13–end
28	Sa	Num. 11. 16–17, 24–29	1 Cor. ch. 2
29	S	THE SEVENTH SUNDAY OF EASTER (Sunday after Ascension Day)	
30	M	Num. 27. 15–end	1 Cor. ch. 3
31	Tu	THE VISITATION	
		Where The Visitation is celebrated on 2 July:	
		1 Sam. 10. 1–10	1 Cor. 12. 1–13

June 2022

1	W	1 Kings 19. 1–18	Matt. 3. 13–end
2	Th	Ezek. 11. 14–20	Matt. 9.35 – 10.20
3	F	Ezek. 36. 22–28	Matt. 12. 22–32
4	Sa	*At Evening Prayer, the readings for the Eve of Pentecost are used. At other services, the following readings are used:*	
		Mic. 3. 1–8	Eph. 6. 10–20
5	S	**PENTECOST** (Whit Sunday)	
6	M	Gen. 12. 1–9	Rom. 4. 13–end
7	Tu	Gen. 13. 1–12	Rom. 12. 9–end
8	W	Gen. ch. 15	Rom. 4. 1–8
9	Th	Gen. 22. 1–18	Heb. 11. 8–19
10	F	Isa. 51. 1–8	John 8. 48–end
11	Sa	BARNABAS	
		At Evening Prayer, the readings for the Eve of Trinity Sunday are used.	

117

12 S **TRINITY SUNDAY**
13 M Exod. 2. 1–10
14 Tu Exod. 2. 11–end Acts 7. 17–29
15 W Exod. 3. 1–12 Acts 7. 30–38
16 Th *Day of Thanksgiving for the Institution of Holy Communion (Corpus Christi), or, where Corpus Christi is celebrated as a Lesser Festival:*
Exod. 6. 1–13 John 9. 24–38
17 F Exod. 34. 1–10 Mark 7. 1–13
18 Sa Exod. 34. 27–end 2 Cor. 3. 7–end
19 S THE FIRST SUNDAY AFTER TRINITY
20 M Gen. 37. 1–11 Rom. 12. 9–21
21 Tu Gen. 41. 15–40 Mark 13. 1–13
22 W Gen. 42. 17–end Matt. 18. 1–14
23 Th Gen. 45. 1–15 Acts 7. 9–16
24 F THE BIRTH OF JOHN THE BAPTIST
25 Sa Gen. 50. 4–21 Luke 15. 11–end
26 S THE SECOND SUNDAY AFTER TRINITY
27 M Isa. ch. 32 Jas. 3. 13–end
28 Tu Prov. 3. 1–18 Matt. 5. 1–12
29 W PETER AND PAUL
30 Th Jer. 6. 9–15 1 Tim. 2. 1–6

July 2022
1 F 1 Sam. 16. 14–end John 14. 15–end
2 Sa Isa. 6. 1–9 Rev. 19. 9–end
3 S THOMAS
or THE THIRD SUNDAY AFTER TRINITY
4 M Exod. 13. 13b–end Luke 15. 1–10
5 Tu Prov. 1. 20–end Jas. 5. 13–end
6 W Isa. 5. 8–24 Jas. 1. 17–25
7 Th Isa. 57. 14–end John 13. 1–17
8 F Jer. 15. 15–end Luke 16. 19–31
9 Sa Isa. 25. 1–9 Acts 2. 22–33
10 S THE FOURTH SUNDAY AFTER TRINITY
11 M Exod. 20. 1–17 Matt. 6. 1–15
12 Tu Prov. 6. 6–19 Luke 4. 1–14
13 W Isa. 24. 1–15 1 Cor. 6. 1–11
14 Th Job ch. 7 Matt. 7. 21–29
15 F Jer. 20. 7–end Matt. 27. 27–44
16 Sa Job ch. 28 Heb. 11.32 – 12.2
17 S THE FIFTH SUNDAY AFTER TRINITY
18 M Exod. 32. 1–14 Col. 3. 1–11
19 Tu Prov. 9. 1–12 2 Thess. 2.13 – 3.5
20 W Isa. 26. 1–9 Rom. 8. 12–27
21 Th Jer. 8.18 – 9.6 John 13. 21–35
22 F MARY MAGDALENE
23 Sa Hos. 11. 1–11 Matt. 28. 1–7
24 S THE SIXTH SUNDAY AFTER TRINITY
25 M JAMES
26 Tu Prov. 11. 1–12 Mark 12. 38–44
27 W Isa. 33. 2–10 Phil. 1. 1–11
28 Th Job ch. 38 Luke 18. 1–14
29 F Job 42. 1–6 John 3. 1–15
30 Sa Eccles. 9. 1–11 Heb. 1. 1–9
31 S THE SEVENTH SUNDAY AFTER TRINITY

August 2022
1 M Num. 23. 1–12 1 Cor. 1. 10–17
2 Tu Prov. 12. 1–12 Gal. 3. 1–14
3 W Isa. 49. 8–13 2 Cor. 8. 1–11
4 Th Hos. ch. 14 John 15. 1–17
5 F 2 Sam. 18. 18–end Matt. 27. 57–66
6 Sa THE TRANSFIGURATION
7 S THE EIGHTH SUNDAY AFTER TRINITY
8 M Joel 3. 16–21 Mark 4. 21–34
9 Tu Prov. 12. 13–end John 1. 43–51
10 W Isa. 55. 8–end 2 Tim. 2. 8–19
11 Th Isa. 38. 1–8 Mark 5. 21–43
12 F Jer. 14. 1–9 Luke 8. 4–15
13 Sa Eccles. 5. 10–19 1 Tim. 6. 6–16
14 S THE NINTH SUNDAY AFTER TRINITY
15 M THE BLESSED VIRGIN MARY

Where the Blessed Virgin Mary is celebrated on 8 September:
Josh. 1. 1–9 1 Cor. 9. 19–end
16 Tu Prov. 15. 1–11 Gal. 2. 15–end
17 W Isa. 49. 1–7 1 John ch. 1
18 Th Prov. 27. 1–12 John 15. 12–27
19 F Isa. 59. 8–end Mark 15. 6–20
20 Sa Zech. 7.8 – 8.8 Luke 20. 27–40
21 S THE TENTH SUNDAY AFTER TRINITY
22 M Judg. 13. 1–23 Luke 10. 38–42
23 Tu Prov. 15. 15–end Matt. 15. 21–28
24 W BARTHOLOMEW
25 Th Jer. 16. 1–15 Luke 12. 35–48
26 F Jer. 18. 1–11 Heb. 1. 1–9
27 Sa Jer. 26. 1–19 Eph. 3. 1–13
28 S THE ELEVENTH SUNDAY AFTER TRINITY
29 M Ruth 2. 1–13 Luke 10. 25–37
30 Tu Prov. 16. 1–11 Phil. 3. 4b–end
31 W Deut. 11. 1–21 2 Cor. 9. 6–end

September 2022
1 Th Ecclus. ch. 2 John 16. 1–15
or Eccles. 2. 12–25
2 F Obad. 1–10 John 19. 1–16
3 Sa 2 Kings 2. 11–14 Luke 24. 36–end
4 S THE TWELFTH SUNDAY AFTER TRINITY
5 M 1 Sam. 17. 32–50 Matt. 8. 14–22
6 Tu Prov. 17. 1–15 Luke 7. 1–17
7 W Jer. 5. 20–end 2 Pet. 3. 8–end
8 Th Dan. 2. 1–23 Luke 10. 1–20
9 F Dan. 3. 1–28 Rev. ch. 15
10 Sa Dan. ch. 6 Phil. 2. 14–24
11 S THE THIRTEENTH SUNDAY AFTER TRINITY
12 M 2 Sam. 7. 4–17 2 Cor. 5. 1–10
13 Tu Prov. 18. 10–21 Rom. 14. 10–end
14 W HOLY CROSS DAY
15 Th Isa. 49. 14–end John 16. 16–24
16 F Job 9. 1–24 Mark 15. 21–32
17 Sa Exod. 19. 1–9 John 20. 11–18
18 S THE FOURTEENTH SUNDAY AFTER TRINITY
19 M Hagg. ch. 1 Mark 7. 9–23
20 Tu Prov. 21. 1–18 Mark 6. 30–44
21 W MATTHEW
22 Th Lam. 3. 34–48 Rom. 7. 14–end
23 F 1 Kings 19. 4–18 1 Thess. ch. 3
24 Sa Ecclus. 4. 11–28 2 Tim. 3. 10–end
or Deut. 29. 2–15
25 S THE FIFTEENTH SUNDAY AFTER TRINITY
26 M Wisd. 6. 12–21 Matt. 15. 1–9
or Job 12. 1–16
27 Tu Prov. 8. 1–11 Luke 6. 39–end
28 W Prov. 2. 1–15 Col. 1. 9–20
29 Th MICHAEL AND ALL ANGELS
30 F Ecclus. 1. 1–20 1 Cor. 1. 18–end
or Deut. 7. 7–16

October 2022
1 Sa Wisd. 9. 1–12 Luke 2. 41–end
or Jer. 1. 4–10
2 S THE SIXTEENTH SUNDAY AFTER TRINITY
3 M Gen. 21. 1–13 Luke 1. 26–38
4 Tu Ruth 4. 7–17 Luke 2. 25–38
5 W 2 Kings 4. 1–7 John 2. 1–11
6 Th 2 Kings 4. 25b–37 Mark 3. 19b–35
7 F Judith 8. 9–17, 28–36 John 19. 25b–30
or Ruth 1. 1–18
8 Sa Exod. 15. 19–27 Acts 1. 6–14
9 S THE SEVENTEENTH SUNDAY AFTER TRINITY
10 M Exod. 19. 16–end Heb. 12. 18–end
11 Tu 1 Chron. 16. 1–13 Rev. 11. 16–end
12 W 1 Chron. 29. 10–19 Col. 3. 12–17
13 Th Neh. 8. 1–12 1 Cor. 14. 1–12
14 F Isa. 1. 10–17 Mark 12. 28–34

15	Sa	Dan. 6. 6–23	Rev. 12. 7–12
16	S	THE EIGHTEENTH SUNDAY AFTER TRINITY	
17	M	2 Sam. 22. 4–7, 17–20	Heb. 7.26 – 8.6
18	Tu	LUKE	
19	W	Hos. ch. 14	Jas. 2. 14–26
20	Th	Isa. 24. 1–15	John 16. 25–33
21	F	Jer. 14. 1–9	Luke 23. 44–56
22	Sa	Zech. 8. 14–end	John 20. 19–end
23	S	THE LAST SUNDAY AFTER TRINITY	
24	M	Isa. 42. 14–21	Luke 1. 5–25
25	Tu	1 Sam. 4. 12–end	Luke 1. 57–80
26	W	Baruch ch. 5	Mark 1. 1–11
		or Hagg. 1. 1–11	
27	Th	Isa. ch. 35	Matt. 11. 2–19
28	F	SIMON AND JUDE	
29	Sa	Isa. 43. 15–21	Acts 19. 1–10

If All Saints' Day is celebrated on Sunday 30 October, the readings for the Eve of All Saints' are used at Evening Prayer.

30	S	THE FOURTH SUNDAY BEFORE ADVENT	
31	M	*At Evening Prayer, the readings for the Eve of All Saints are used. At other services, the following readings are used:*	
		Esther 3. 1–11; 4. 7–17	Matt. 18. 1–10

November 2022

| 1 | Tu | ALL SAINTS' DAY | |

or, where All Saints' Day is celebrated on Sunday 30 October:

		Ezek. 18. 21–end	Matt. 18. 12–20
2	W	Prov. 3. 27–end	Matt. 18. 21–end
3	Th	Exod. 23. 1–9	Matt. 19. 1–15
4	F	Prov. 3. 13–18	Matt. 19. 16–end
5	Sa	Deut. 28. 1–6	Matt. 20. 1–16
6	S	THE THIRD SUNDAY BEFORE ADVENT	
7	M	Isa. 40. 21–end	Rom. 11. 25–end
8	Tu	Ezek. 34. 20–end	John 10. 1–18
9	W	Lev. 26. 3–13	Titus 2. 1–10
10	Th	Hos. 6. 1–6	Matt. 9. 9–13
11	F	Mal. ch. 4	John 4. 5–26
12	Sa	Mic. 6. 6–8	Col. 3. 12–17
13	S	THE SECOND SUNDAY BEFORE ADVENT	
14	M	Mic. 7. 1–7	Matt. 10. 24–39
15	Tu	Hab. 3. 1–19a	1 Cor. 4. 9–16
16	W	Zech. 8. 1–13	Mark 13. 3–8
17	Th	Zech. 10. 6–end	1 Pet. 5. 1–11
18	F	Mic. 4. 1–5	Luke 9. 28–36
19	Sa	*At Evening Prayer, the readings for the Eve of Christ the King are used. At other services, the following readings are used:*	

		Exod. 16. 1–21	John 6. 3–15
20	S	CHRIST THE KING (The Sunday next before Advent)	
21	M	Jer. 30. 1–3, 10–17	Rom. 12. 9–21
22	Tu	Jer. 30. 18–24	John 10. 22–30
23	W	Jer. 31. 1–9	Matt. 15. 21–31
24	Th	Jer. 31. 10–17	Matt. 16. 13–end
25	F	Jer. 31. 31–37	Heb. 10. 11–18
26	Sa	Isa. 51.17 – 52.2	Eph. 5. 1–20
27	S	THE FIRST SUNDAY OF ADVENT	
28	M	Mal. 3. 1–6	Matt. 3. 1–6
29	Tu	Zeph. 3. 14–end	1 Thess. 4. 13–end
30	W	ANDREW	

December 2022

1	Th	Mic. 5. 2–5a	John 3. 16–21
2	F	Isa. 66. 18–end	Luke 13. 22–30
3	Sa	Mic. 7. 8–15	Rom. 15.30 – 16.7, 25–end
4	S	THE SECOND SUNDAY OF ADVENT	
5	M	Jer. 7. 1–11	Phil. 4. 4–9
6	Tu	Dan. 7. 9–14	Matt. 24. 15–28
7	W	Amos 9. 11–end	Rom. 13. 8–14
8	Th	Jer. 23. 5–8	Mark 11. 1–11
9	F	Jer. 33. 14–22	Luke 21. 25–36
10	Sa	Zech. 14. 4–11	Rev. 22. 1–7
11	S	THE THIRD SUNDAY OF ADVENT	
12	M	Isa. 40. 1–11	Matt. 3. 1–12
13	Tu	Lam. 3. 22–33	1 Cor. 1. 1–9
14	W	Joel 3. 9–16	Matt. 24. 29–35
15	Th	Isa. ch. 62	1 Thess. 3. 6–13
16	F	Isa. 2. 1–5	Acts 11. 1–18
17	Sa	Ecclus. 224. 1–9	1 Cor. 2. 1–13
		or Prov. 8. 22–31	
18	S	THE FOURTH SUNDAY OF ADVENT	
19	M	Isa. 11. 1–9	Rom. 15. 7–13
20	Tu	Isa. 22. 21–23	Rev. 3. 7–13
21	W	Num. 24. 15b–19	Rev. 22. 10–21
22	Th	Jer. 30. 7–11a	Acts 4. 1–12
23	F	Isa. 7. 10–15	Matt. 1. 18–23
24	Sa	*At Evening Prayer, the readings for Christmas Eve are used. At other services, the following readings are used:*	
		Isa. 29. 13–18	1 John 4. 7–16
25	S	CHRISTMAS DAY	
26	M	STEPHEN	
27	Tu	JOHN THE EVANGELIST	
28	W	THE HOLY INNOCENTS	
29	Th	Mic. 1. 1–4; 2. 12–13	Luke 2. 1–7
30	F	Isa. 9. 2–7	John 8. 12–20
31	Sa	Eccles. 3. 1–13	Rev. 21. 1–8

CALENDAR 2022

CALENDAR 2023

CALENDAR 2022 — legend

- A = Ash Wednesday, Ascension, Advent
- A⁻ = Before Advent
- A⁻¹ = also All Saints, 2022 and 2023 (if transferred)
- A⁻¹ = Christ the King
- An = Annunciation
- AS = All Saints
- B = Baptism
- E = Epiphany, Easter
- E¹ = also Presentation, 2022 and 2023 (if transferred)
- G = Good Friday
- L = Lent
- L⁻ = Before Lent

CALENDAR 2023 — legend

- M = Maundy Thursday
- P = Palm Sunday
- Pr = Presentation
- T = Trinity
- (T¹ = also Thomas, 2022)
- (T⁶ = also Transfiguration, 2023)
- T⁻ = Last Sunday after Trinity
- W = Pentecost (Whit Sunday)
- X = Christmas